Along the Santa Fe Trail

ALONG THE
Santa Fe Trail

PHOTOGRAPHS BY
Joan Myers

ESSAY BY
Marc Simmons

University of New Mexico Press
ALBUQUERQUE

Library of Congress Cataloging in Publication Data

Myers, Joan, 1944–

   Along the Santa Fe Trail.

   Bibliography: p.
   Includes index.
   1. Santa Fé Trail.   2. Southwest, New—History—
1848–   . 3. Southwest, New—Description and
travel—1981–   . 4. Myers, Joan, 1944–   —
Journeys—Santa Fé Trail. I. Simmons, Marc.   II.
Title.
F786.M98   1986   978   86–6928
ISBN 0-8263-0881-3
ISBN 0-8263-0882-1 (pbk.)

Plates printed in Japan

Second printing, 1989

Contents

Plates

To Les, David, Denise, and Valerie,
who walked the Trail in '84.

—Marc Simmons

Acknowledgments

IN MY YEARS OF PROWLING up and down the length of the Santa Fe Trail, I have been assisted in my searches for sites and for research materials by many dedicated history buffs and trail hounds. For help in Missouri, I owe a large debt to Pauline (Polly) Fowler of Independence, Sylvia Mooney, Raytown, and William Goff, Kansas City. Kansans who provided special aid are the late Amelia J. Betts and Katharine Kelley of Baldwin City, Roe Groom at Council Grove, and Bill Pitts, Ruth Olson, and Earl Monger, all of the Santa Fe Trail Center, Larned. Jesse Scott, Jr., Garden City, shared his maps and extensive knowledge of the lower reaches of the Mountain Branch of the trail. Farmer Paul Bentrup, Deerfield, Kansas, who has generously donated ten acres of trail ruts to his local historical society, provided many bits of information on the route in western Kansas and eastern Colorado that I would otherwise have missed. In New Mexico, Homer Hastings, former superintendent of Fort Union National Monument, gave Joan Myers and myself a special tour of historic sites in the La Junta area. Finally, I wish to thank the staff of the University of New Mexico Press, especially editor David Holtby, for their dedicated effort on behalf of this project.

—MARC SIMMONS

For the men in my life:
my husband Gary; and my children,
Julian, Raymond, Rob, and Scott.

—Joan Myers

Photographer's Note

IN OCTOBER 1981, I WAS ASKED to join the New Mexico Photographic Survey. This project, funded in part by the National Endowment for the Arts, provided small grants to twelve photographers who were commissioned to photograph a subject of their choice within the state.

I had long been intrigued by the wide plains and volcanic landscape of northeastern New Mexico. In looking at my state highway map for that area, I found a thin dotted line that marked the location of the long-abandoned Santa Fe Trail. With my finger I followed it as it passed through Cañoncito, Pecos, San Miguel, Fort Union, Wagon Mound, and many miles of unknown country. I wondered, what would I photograph? The trail had not been used for over a hundred years, and only a few historical photographs survived to document the major forts and small New Mexican towns. No guidebook was then in print. With great enthusiasm but little knowledge of New Mexico history and less of the trail, I declared that I had found my subject for the survey.

I began by reading historical studies and the early journals of Susan Magoffin and Josiah Gregg. Further research revealed several out-of-print guidebooks, early maps, and an abundance of engaging journals by trail travelers. When I finally set off with my camera and traveled to spots on the trail mentioned in the accounts, I found that a surprising number of structures and long miles of the old road's ruts had survived the intervening century of urbanization, cultivation, and neglect.

Gradually I expanded my territory eastward from New Mexico into Oklahoma, Colorado, Kansas, and Missouri, and I continued photographing long after the requirements of the survey grant had been met. In all, I traveled more than 15,000 miles over a three-year period with my 4 × 5 field camera, all too often aware of light fading and miles yet to travel.

I am grateful to many people for their unselfish support and advice. Steven A. Yates, curator of photography at the Museum of Fine Arts in Santa Fe, organized and directed the New Mexico Photographic Survey. His vision initiated the project, and his enthusiasm was a constant encouragement. Marc Simmons had the original idea for this book and the confidence to present it long before he had any idea what my photographs would look like. His hand-drawn maps were invaluable in locating obscure sites. My only regret is that his recently published guidebook, *Following the Santa Fe Trail*, was not available sooner; I would have been spared a few wrong turns. Now anyone who wishes can locate the trail's landmarks.

For the most part, I traveled and photographed alone. I was aided, however, by many individuals along the trail who helped me find early structures and landmarks. Farmers drew me maps in the dirt. Ranchers in their pickups drove me over pasture land to point out old foundations or circled to the top of a mesa for a spectacular view of the trail ruts below. Each person told me the history of his or her small section of the trail, and then often insisted on my stopping for a cup of coffee or a piece of homemade pie. I owe a particular thanks to Pete and Faye Gaines and their granddaughter Krystal at Point of Rocks, New Mexico; to Earl Monger in Larned, Kansas; to Roe Groom in Council Grove, Kansas; and to Pauline Fowler in Independence, Missouri. My photographs are a small memory of special people and a great adventure.

—JOAN MYERS

Preface

SOME WORD IS IN ORDER concerning how this book came about. But to tell that, I must explain something of myself and my personal relationship with history. Only then will it be clear how I became so closely, even passionately involved with a subject like the Santa Fe Trail.

Almost as far back as I can remember, I have been fascinated by the history of the American Southwest. As a youngster I started reading and collecting books on the area, and later, after delving deeply into primary historical sources, I began writing my own books and teaching. Yet, even that was not quite enough to still my craving to know more about the past. Twenty years ago, I built my own Spanish-style adobe house in the Galisteo Basin southeast of Santa Fe. Its dirt floor and lack of modern conveniences gave meaning to the definition of "roughing it," but the hardships I considered minor, especially since the lack of twentieth-century encumbrances allowed me to live economically and work, in isolation, uninterrupted.

Friends accused me of wanting to turn back the clock, a charge I have consistently denied. I entertain no desire to experience the Indian raids, smallpox epidemics, and poverty of books that characterized life on the southwestern frontier. But while I may not wish to see the clock turned back, I don't mind winding it up again. That is to say, a vicarious retreat into the past in search of what is interesting, useful, and entertaining I find a perfectly acceptable activity, even when practically everyone else is stretching his neck toward the future and the far horizon of the Computer Age.

Voyaging back on the seas of history possesses certain natural advantages not available to the people who actually made that history. Through reading and travel I can get in touch with the past without facing the risk of those raids and epidemics. I'm not restricted to any one period or place but can range at will across continents and centuries. I can be highly selective in the company I keep, singling out for friendship some of the most intriguing personalities ever to walk the globe. And, finally, when weary of exploration in dark corners of the long ago, I can always step quickly back into the present. Yes, the whole experience has much to recommend it.

But now what about the Santa Fe Trail? I did not set out to become an authority on that subject; it occurred almost by accident. For many years, my writing and research had focused mainly on the Spanish colonial period in the Southwest, a slice of history filled with movement and high drama. Occasionally, I did stray into the era that followed, dealing with events attendant upon the American arrival in the region. And that had led to my authoring several articles, including one for an encyclopedia, on the history of the Santa Fe Trail.

Then, in 1978 an editor with the National Geographic Society contacted me and asked if I would be willing to write a chapter on the Santa Fe Trail for one of their new books to be called *Trails West*. Well-known authorities had already been enlisted to cover the Oregon, Mormon, California, Gila, and Bozeman trails. But, as the editor explained, no scholar could be found who qualified as a specialist on the Santa Fe Trail. Since I had some experience in the area, albeit limited, perhaps I could bone up and do the job.

The offer presented an exciting challenge and a chance to explore an aspect of western history that to date I had only surveyed superficially. And, my deficiencies in background I knew could be quickly overcome by a crash reading program in literature of the trail. Perhaps most enticing was the prospect of a drive over the Santa Fe Trail, from its head in central Missouri to its finish in New Mexico. That was absolutely required, the editor had explained, so that I could gather first-hand experiences and impressions that would lend the weight of authority to my chapter. The society would foot my expenses.

Now, I had read of the famous campsites and landmarks strung along the one-thousand-mile length of the trail and knew that their names, in proper succession, had been committed to memory by all early-day wagon travelers. But they had remained for me only lifeless place names on a page. Driving the trail today—which is possible because much of the old route is closely paralleled by modern highways—would give me a look at those historic sites, something I had not taken the time or trouble to do before. So assessing everything, it was easy to accept the society's offer.

I made my trip over the trail in August of that year; delved deeply into contemporary journals, diaries, and newspaper accounts; and, wrote up and submitted my chapter with some dispatch. In the normal course of events, that would have ended my association with the Santa Fe Trail, and I would have promptly returned to my prowlings in Spanish colonial vineyards. But that was not the way it worked out. I was not done with the trail, and the realization began to dawn slowly that I never would be.

During the short term encompassing my travels, research, and writing, I had become a hopeless Santa Fe Trail addict. The old pioneer road had laid hold of my affections with a vicelike grip, and it seemed beyond my power to loosen it, even if I'd wanted to. In the modern trail I had found something living and organic, rooted far in the past and yet still clinging to life in the afterpart of the twentieth century. Why this should be true posed something of a mystery, one that had escaped notice but whose effects could be clearly discerned if not immediately interpreted. Moreover, I perceived there at the beginning that the trail and all the events that had swirled around it were filled with little lessons shedding slanted rays of light on the human condition. An 1850s traveler, finishing a crossing of the prairies, wrote in her journal, "The blue sky above me had been bread and meat for my soul. The trail had become my point of outlook upon the universe." Once my addiction was complete, I knew exactly what was meant.

It came as something of a surprise, and to this day it remains for me a subject of wonderment, when I began to meet others who had been over the Santa Fe Trail and who, to a greater or lesser degree, had also become confirmed trail addicts. Most had driven, in modern cars with air-conditioning and tape decks. But others had taken more primitive means, going by foot, horseback, covered wagon, or bicycle. For the fact is that while trail travel was supposed to have come to an end in early 1880, with the arrival of the railroad in Santa Fe, there are people still who refuse to heed the message.

They cannot bear to let the Santa Fe Trail slip away into the great silent ocean of history, and so they continue to follow the fading wagon tracks in pursuit of an experience that is never quite brought to completion. Out there beyond the Mississippi and across the wide Missouri in a land of pancake plains, sky-touching mountains, and sage-studded plateaus the westering trail to Santa Fe can still capture the imagination and command the devotion of those who, approaching too close, fall prey to its siren call.

The book in hand represents a distillation of what I have learned about the Santa Fe Trail during my years of close association with it. It is not "a history" in the usual definition of that term, but it does deal in a wider sense with things historical. The book focuses on connections, the interweaving of the past with the present that goes on constantly and influences us whether we are aware of it or not. As one person's encounter with one narrow aspect of our nation's story, the book's scope may seem parochial, but at least some of the questions that it addresses reach beyond the bounds of regionalism.

The tone and mood of my words take their cue from the photographs of Joan Myers. Like myself, she has done a good amount of rambling along the trail, soaking up what the colonial Spaniards would have called its *ambiente,* the atmosphere or feel of the thing in all its multifaceted dimensions. It was she who conceived of this book, enlisted me in the partnership, and provided the necessary spur that kept the project moving toward its end.

I preceded Joan into the separate world that encompasses Santa Fe Trail studies. Her own introduction came several years ago when she was asked by the Museum of New Mexico to join other distinguished photographers in preparing an exhibit on southwestern themes. By merest chance, she drew the topic of the Santa Fe Trail. Knowing little about it and unsure where to find trail points of interest that could be photographed, she made inquiries and was directed to me.

I heard her out and then explained where she might go in northeastern New Mexico to get the pictures that were to comprise her part of the exhibit. The whole thing wouldn't take very long, a matter of a few weeks at most. But that was sufficient time on the trail, I knew, to pose a serious danger, and I issued a warning.

"Be advised," I said, "of a powerful spell that hangs over the Santa Fe Trail. It creeps up on you unaware, grabs you from behind, and you are beyond rescue. Victims innumerable have succumbed. Symptomatic of the spell is an imperishable longing to be constantly on the trail, moving back and forth, from landmark to landmark between Missouri and New Mexico. The incessant tug is always there, pulling you away from home, family, friends, and your proper business. It is a malady of mind, a compulsion, a raging addiction. Thus far, no cure has been discovered. The best course is to be forewarned and take rigorous precautions to avoid infection."

Joan Myers, being of sound intellect and steady temperament, thought perhaps I was unbalanced. I'm sure at the outset she regarded her small assignment as in no way beyond the ordinary, and certainly not one that would engage her attention a single moment longer than necessary. My ominous warning, pronounced with rigorous sincerity, fell, therefore, on deaf ears.

Although I make no claims to the office of prophet, in this case I had struck the mark with unerring aim. A month or more elapsed before I saw Joan again. In that period, she had ventured onto the trail, twice, and five minutes conversation was enough to convince me that she had tumbled over the edge. Joan Myers had become an unredeemable Santa Fe Trail addict. The ranks of the hopeless had gained another new recruit.

In the many crossings of the trail Joan has made since that time, she has assembled an impressive collection of photographic prints that captures the magic and charm which cling with a kind of stark reality to the modern skirts of the

Santa Fe Trail. My narrative is designed to complement her visual images and to expand upon the theme suggested in them—that the old trail, rich in human experience, retains the capacity to touch something deep and vital in man's hidden self. In another sense, this book may be seen as a tribute, as a small but lovingly crafted monument, designed by writer and photographer to honor that grand and ageless lady, known to history and to all romantic adventurers as . . . THE SANTA FE TRAIL.

Los Cerrillos, New Mexico   MARC SIMMONS

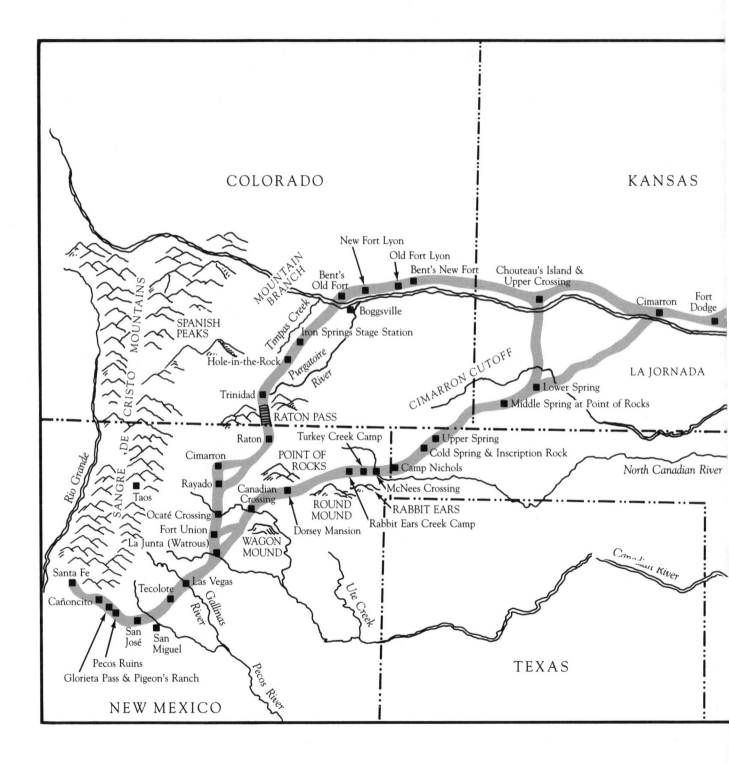

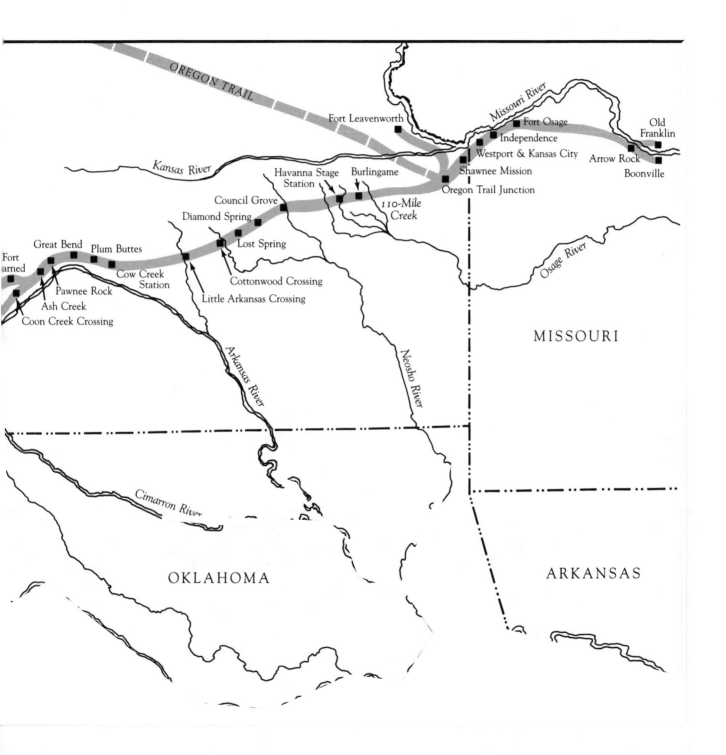

Along the Santa Fe Trail

Say, pard, have you sighted a schooner
A hittin' the Santa Fe Trail.
They made it here Monday or sooner
With a water keg roped on the rail.

But I guess I'll make Cedars by sundown
And campin' may be in a swale.
I'll come to a gal on a pinto
Alongside the Santa Fe Trail.

from a popular song

ONE

A
Beginning
at Franklin

IT WAS HOT AND I WAS UNHAPPY ABOUT IT. Early June and already the heat in the Missouri River bottoms was staggering, while the muggy air, thick as hospital gauze, seemed barely fit for breathing. With the high humidity, the river muck had that pungent, fishy smell associated with ocean wharves. Having lived long in the arid Southwest, this damp, wooded country of the East seemed to me uninhabitable. But I had come with a firm purpose, to stand in the village of Franklin at the very head of the Santa Fe Trail, so I fanned myself with a road map and resolved to ignore the discomfort.

Almost in the center of Missouri, I had left Interstate 70 at the Boonville exit. Two miles more brought me to Boonville itself where I drove down a tidy main street lined with nineteenth-century storefronts. At the far edge of downtown, traffic was funneled onto a narrow, antique bridge stretching a quarter mile across the wide and muddy river. In the way of safety, the structure looked entirely unreliable, but since Franklin lay on the other side I had little choice but to go ahead. At once steel girders began to rattle and shake, and I was struck with the uneasy thought that they could give way at any moment sending my car hurtling a hundred feet into the slate gray water below. But that dark prospect was quickly overshadowed by another, for looming in front was a huge truck approaching in the opposite lane. Measuring its girth by eye and assessing the narrowness of the bridge, I doubted there was room enough for us to pass. But we did, with only inches to spare.

I departed that bridge with an overwhelming sense of relief vowing to avoid it in the future. Yet, that was to prove beyond my doing since I was shortly to discover the lure of Franklin irresistible. Although I had no inkling of it then, I would return year after year to renew acquaintance with the land and the river where the Santa Fe Trail had its birth. That became an imperative, I learned, because to know and understand the men who betook themselves to New Mexico in great merchant caravans, one has to come here and absorb the atmosphere of the place by degrees, braving summer's smothering temperatures or the razor sharp winds of winter that slice through the Missouri breaks.

In spite of my best efforts that day, I was not able to pinpoint exactly the location of the first Franklin, the one now referred to in books as Old Franklin. After making a brief splash as the town that opened the Santa Fe trade, it disappeared by sections into the maw of a flood-swollen river. A musket shot beyond the north end of the Boonville bridge, I found one of the handsome granite trail markers placed in 1909 and inscribed "Old Franklin." It was the first of nearly two hundred such commemorative stones that members of the Daughters of the American Revolution, in a burst of patriotic fervor, scattered all along the old route to Santa Fe.

As nearly as possible the conscientious Daughters attempted to locate their markers, trailside, with historical exactness. They studied documents in libraries and archives and consulted persons still living—it then being the early twentieth century—who had first-hand knowledge of communities now gone and of the trail now mostly faded away. Their undertaking, therefore, had much to recommend it in the way of authenticity.

Still, about the location of this Old Franklin stone, I at first entertained some doubts. The original town, founded in 1817, was close to the river—too close, we know now. A municipal map, dating from the community's short heyday and labeled with some presumption, "City of Franklin" shows house lots platted at the river's edge. That would have placed the town limits some distance southwest of the Daughters' marker and upstream from the Boonville bridge. In fact, as I later learned, traces of foundations had been found a quarter mile in that direction.

So there it lay, in sight of the marker: Old Franklin, where visionary individuals of nineteenth-century mind, driven either by economic necessity or a thirst for adventure, initially took to the Santa Fe Trail. For a tiny interval in the long sweep of our westward movement, Franklin sparkled in the sun, attracting ambitious men the way a tallow candle drew fluttering moths.

Many of those men had come out of Tennessee, Kentucky, Virginia, and the Carolinas, and some even from the northeastern states. Among them were hard-scrabble farmers whose aim reached no further than taking up a swatch of silt-rich Missouri bottomlands and scratching out a living. But for numbers of others, who were full of enterprise and possessed of some culture, Franklin stood on the cutting-edge of America's expansive frontier. It offered excitement, opportunity, the chance to be out front, and some prospect of material gain—in short, those things mainstream Americans still turn their sights upon.

I scanned the alluvial floodplain, checkered now with tilled fields and bounded by powerlines and wire fences and tried to picture it as things were when Franklin was struggling to get a toehold and raw wilderness lay all around. This part of Missouri then was known as the "Boone's Lick" country, after a saline spring or "lick" ten miles upstream from Franklin. There, beginning in 1805 Nathan and Daniel Morgan Boone, sons of the coonskin-bonneted Daniel Boone, took to making salt by boiling down the briny water in huge cast-iron kettles. Where Boones led others were sure to follow. Within a few years settlers from St. Louis and St. Charles had scattered through the neighboring lowlands, carving out farms and raising at strategic points stockade forts to fend off marauding Osage, Quapaw, and Sauk and Fox Indians.

By the time Franklin was organized in 1817—taking its name from Benjamin Franklin—a respectable colony of pioneer folk already had firm roots in the Boone's Lick region. The new town, if providence cooperated, bid fair to become a booming supply and trade center. As an early-day historian rhapsodized: "It had sprung into opulence on the banks of the turbulent Missouri as if a magician had waved his magic wand over the wilderness."

One product of that magic was the appearance, a scant year after Franklin's founding, of the *Missouri Intelligencer*, the strongest and most renowned pioneer newspaper west of St. Louis. An early issue proclaimed that "immigration to this territory exceeds almost belief," and it calculated that 271 wagons were currently on the road bearing no fewer than 3,000 persons toward new homes in the Franklin district. "We will soon possess a vast population," the *Intelligencer* editorialized gleefully. It was the timeless prediction of men who fiercely believed that expansion and growth are certain roadmarks leading to progress and the good life.

Signs of Franklin's opulence, besides its newspaper office, included 120 log houses, several two-story frame buildings, two brick buildings (the bricks costing $10 a thousand), 13 stores, 4 taverns serving rum and Monongahela whiskey, 2 blacksmith shops, 2 imposing steam mills, 2 billiard rooms, a courthouse, log jail, and post office. And all of this existed even before the opening of the Santa Fe Trail catapulted Franklin to new prominence.

Yet, the seeds of disaster had been sown on day one of the community's founding. As Major Stephen Long observed in 1819, steaming upriver on a scientific expedition, the place known as Franklin was not wisely located. Someday, he opined, it would fall victim to the currents and be carried away. His prophecy was not long in being fulfilled.

The winter of 1825–26 produced an especially heavy snowpack in the Rockies surrounding the headwaters of the Missouri. Rains of spring and early summer swelled the river's overload so that a thin lake spread across the Franklin bottoms while the rush of the main current progressively gouged away the soil bed upon which the town rested. By flood season's end the better part of Franklin had tumbled into the rapacious waters.

Farms on the adjacent flats were also lost. The most spectacular damage was suffered by the learned John Hardeman, who had created amid the customary fields and orchards a ten-acre cultural oasis in the form of an Elizabethan garden replete with ornamental plants and trees imported from around the world. The Missouri claimed more than 650 acres of his celebrated Fruitage Farm and left him in severe financial straits.

When the flood receded many residents, now wiser, moved north two and a half miles to higher ground. They laid out and built New Franklin which, being so far from normal river traffic, promptly slipped into permanent obscurity. An outlying section of Old Franklin, it seems, was spared the worst of the 1826 inundation and hung on well into the 1830s. But the fickleness of the river in springtime eventually forced all hold-outs to leave. At least one two-story house was dismantled brick by brick and reassembled in New Franklin where it stands to this day. Other structures were broken up and carried piecemeal by ferry across river to newly flourishing Boonville, which enjoyed an advantageous location atop a high bluff.

One of my return visits was made in late spring when the Missouri was out of its banks, and I saw firsthand the conditions that caused Franklin to founder. The Old Franklin marker at the foot of the bridge and the Kit Carson Motel and a store across the road were out of the water but not much else. Frame farmhouses in the distance looked like floating barges. Owners sat on their porches with a pole and fishing line cast over the rail.

That trip I was hoping to visit a historic home, Cedar Grove, part of which was reputed to have been built as early as 1827. At the Old Franklin marker I veered off on a state road leading northwest toward Boone's Lick. Within a half mile the pavement suddenly disappeared under a new-formed lake. I slammed on the brakes and stared. A man in a battered pick-up came out of a side road and stopped.

"You can go ahead, if you're of a mind. It's only two or three inches deep. But another foot is headin' down from Nebraska so you'd better come back by evenin'."

He talked as though there was a possibility I might actually drive into that vast lagoon. How that could be done with any hope of staying on the paved road was beyond my comprehension. So, I merely replied, "No thanks! Believe I'll try something else."

Back at the marker junction, I inquired at the Kit Carson Motel. It had been closed for a number of years and water lapped at the foundations of the outermost cabins. Ninety-three-year-old Bertha Carson Amick, a direct descendant of one of Kit's brothers, was living in what had been the motel office.

"Cedar Grove? Yes, I know where that is. It's not far on the way to Boone's Lick. But the main road is under water," she said, speaking in a thin, reedy voice. That was truly the case, I acknowledged.

"I will call my daughter-in-law," said Mrs. Carson Amick. "We'll drive you to Cedar Grove by a rough back route that's still open."

And they did. We headed north toward New Franklin, the slightly elevated cement road resembling for all the world a causeway across an inland bay. Many of the distressed houses we passed had signs out front reading, "Fish For Sale." That seemed to offer the only small means to profit from this watery disaster. Climbing forty or fifty feet out of the floodplain to New Franklin, we picked up a rutted gravel road that carried us in a loop to an upper stretch of the Boone's Lick highway. Shortly afterward we found Cedar Grove, secure on an island of elevated land but overlooking the submerged fields skirting the Missouri. Somewhere down-stream under all that water lay the site of Old Franklin, toppled from its rightful place in the sun by a river that was no respecter of its own banks or of man's attempts to become too close a neighbor.

Before Franklin's demise, however, a wholly unanticipated event placed the town in the forefront of activity on the nation's frontier. That occurrence was local settler William Becknell's inaugural ride to Santa Fe in 1821 with a packtrain of Yankee merchandise. His daring and initiative opened the history of a splendid trail and spawned a grand adventure that would take decades to run its full course. And because of what he started, of course, I was here.

Just who was William Becknell and what combination of imagination, industry, and luck vaulted him into the role of "Father of the Santa Fe Trail?" For a long while little was known of the man's personal history beyond the several journeys he made in the 1820s to New Mexico. But recently a young scholar from Dallas, Larry Beachum, has written a biography of Becknell that allows us to round out the story.

Virginia-born, about 1787, pioneer William Becknell first showed up in the Boone's Lick country of central Missouri in April of 1812. Soon after, he joined a company of U.S. Mounted Rangers to fight Indians, and, as Beachum tells us, he served two adventurous years in units commanded by members of the family of Daniel Boone. Mustered out of the rangers in 1815, he entered into a series of business ventures including involvement in the salt trade at the lick and operation of a ferry service on the Missouri. By 1817 or so, he and his family were residents of Franklin where a plat, preserved in the Missouri state archives, shows him in possession of two house lots scarcely a block from the central public square.

Yet, all was not well with Becknell's life and fortunes. There is every likelihood he was contentious by nature. At least we know that in the heat of early summer 1818, he got in a brawl with one James Riggs, thrashed him royally, and ended up in Circuit Court on an assault charge. Though pleading not guilty, he was fined five dollars. He suffered another personal setback when, entering politics in 1820, he came in last in a race for the new State House of Representatives.

More serious were financial troubles which had begun to plague him as well as his Franklin neighbors. The unbridled activities of land boomers, speculators, and bank creditors had erupted in the Panic of 1819. That crash dealt its hardest blow to frontier states like Missouri, where farmers and small town merchants, caught in a web of debt, were unable to obtain new credit. While the rest of the country bounced back rapidly, these luckless souls flailed desperately over the next several years to keep their heads above the quicksands of bankruptcy.

In the economic crises William Becknell took out several personal loans. Unable to repay, he was arrested for debt on May 29, 1821, by a deputy sheriff. Fortunately, a friend posted $400 bond releasing him, until his trial at least, from humiliating confinement in the county jail. His situation, however, remained precarious. In a land which only that year had achieved statehood and which still reeled from the effects of the crash, and where hard money was as scarce as optimism about the future, how could he restore his solvency and salvage a tarnished name? The answer, as he was soon to learn, lay nearly a thousand miles to the west in a town—Santa Fe—whose very name evoked images of adventure, romance, wealth, and assorted marvels.

Precisely what advice from friends or what bits of news reaching his ears may have prompted William Becknell to organize a trading expedition beyond the western limits of Missouri is a matter yet to be uncovered. In a general way, it can be said that he knew what his contemporaries in Franklin knew about the prospects for an overland commerce. It was common knowledge, for example, that New Mexico as a colony of Spain was closed to outsiders. The Mother Country kept a tight rein, indeed a stranglehold, on the economies of her New World possessions. She wanted no foreigners bearing cheaper goods to encroach upon the monopoly of her own merchants.

In the years prior to 1820 several small parties of Americans had tried to get a foot inside the door of New Mexico, it being so remote from the center of government at Mexico City, they reasoned, that surely enforcement of trade restrictions must be lax. That miscalculation landed most of them in dark, lice-infested dungeons. Their interest in a Santa Fe trade had been kindled by Lieutenant Zebulon Pike's book, published in 1810, concerning his observations while a prisoner in Spanish hands. Exploring the southwest corner of the Louisiana Purchase a few years earlier, he had strayed into New Mexico, suffering arrest and a brief internment in Santa Fe and Chihuahua before being released. All manufactured goods in those northern Spanish provinces, wrote Pike, were scarce and exorbitant in cost. The colonists were hungry for cheap goods, especially textiles and hardware. If Missourians could get around the trade barriers imposed by Spain, a market of considerable magnitude awaited them behind the deserts and rock-ribbed mountains of the far Southwest.

Debt-ridden and with no other prospects in sight, William Becknell's bold ride to Santa Fe in the summer of 1821 was a gamble in desperation, Larry Beachum concludes. Be that as it may, the gamble was far from a long shot. Rumblings were being heard all along the Missouri border that Mexico was in the throes of achieving independence, and, should that come about, the expectation was that Americans would promptly be admitted to New Mexico. Becknell merely bet that his timing was right, that he would be the first one allowed in.

Earliest word of his plans saw light in the pages of the *Missouri Intelligencer* on June 25. Therein, he issued a call for seventy men interested in forming a company to head westward for the purpose of trading horses and mules and "catching Wild Animals of every description." Although Becknell makes no mention of New Mexico, significantly he declared that the party would travel "as far as we wish to go." Caution seems to have persuaded him to disguise his ultimate destination.

In the end, far fewer than seventy enlisted for the journey. Accounts vary. From as few as three or four to as many as seventeen persons may have accompanied Becknell on his history-making trip. For that is what it turned out to be. Moving a few miles upriver to the vicinity of Boone's Lick, they crossed the Missouri by ferry to Arrow Rock and there picked up the Osage Trace, an old trail leading to the outer border of the state. Angling across the entire length of what would later become the state of Kansas, cutting the corner of Colorado, and negotiating the breath-taking heights of Raton Pass, men and pack mules arrived at last in Santa Fe.

To their delight, they discovered that Mexico, indeed, had managed to launch itself on the independent sea of nationhood. New Mexico's Governor Facundo Melgares greeted them warmly, gave them freedom to trade, and announced that all Americans would be welcome. It was precisely the news Becknell needed to guarantee a reversal of his recent ill luck. Promptly he sold out his small stock of goods, loaded the mules with rawhide bundles of Mexican silver coin, and turned his face toward home.

The return was made by a more direct route which avoided the heights of Raton Pass but led through a bleak desert north of the Cimarron River. Becknell was already planning a new venture to Santa Fe, one that could be made by wagon, and the road he now discovered seemed entirely suitable for wheeled traffic. Back in Franklin by late January of 1822, he must have made a triumphal entry. One local tradition holds that stepping from his mount he slit open the hide packs and permitted a shower of bright coins to clink on the pavement and roll into the stone gutters.

Whether at that precise moment William Becknell realized the full significance of what he had done, or whether the certain knowledge of his accomplishment came later in that year of 1822, following his round trip to Santa Fe with a small train of three freight wagons—the first crossing of the Great Plains by caravan— has not been recorded. In pioneering the trail to New Mexico, he not only lifted himself out of debt and showed his hard-pressed neighbors how to do the same, but he also allowed Missouri to begin its escape from the economic doldrums and an unnatural dependency on the eastern states.

That was not all that his initiative set in motion. In spite of its impressive volume of trade, which would eventually climb to a million dollars a year in receipts, the Santa Fe Trail was of almost equal significance in helping to shape the conception Americans of that day had of the far side of the continent. A public that responded warmly to the romantic frontier depicted by James Fenimore Cooper and Washington Irving was eager to read the latest newspaper accounts or published journals of men who risked an overland journey to carry on commerce in a foreign land. Their inevitable tales of Indian fights, buffalo hunts, prairie fires, rattlesnakes, and lightning strikes, fording rain-swollen streams and at-tending Spanish fandangos at trail's end all appealed strongly to the popular imagination. And such yarn-spinning helped create the image of the Great West as an appropriate theater of opportunity toward which adventurous and enter-prising men could direct their energies.

Further, the Santa Fe traders who followed Becknell's first wagon tracks helped dispel, in some measure, the illusion of a Great American Desert lying beyond the tall grass prairies and below the tag end of the Rockies. For them New Mexico became a kind of Canaan, in economic terms anyway. One bit of early trail doggerel aptly expressed their sentiments in that regard:

> So hold your horses, Billy,
> Just hold them for a day
> I've crossed the River Jordan
> And I'm bound for Santa Fe.

By crossing the Jordan, American merchants, wagon masters, and teamsters entered the Promised Land and continued on to the new Jerusalem at Santa Fe. In the eyes of many, reality failed to live up to the dream and the promise: instead of the expected gleaming palace and residences of stone in proper Hispanic style, they found public buildings and humble homes made of unfired adobe brick and crudely adzed timbers. Much of the populace was beggarly and vermin-ridden. Local government was corrupt and entirely capricious when it came to the collection of tariffs on goods imported from the United States.

Still, not all of the luster faded. Profits *could* be made, even if at times that meant selling at wholesale to New Mexican entrepreneurs who freighted American merchandise southward to the richer silver-mining towns of Chihuahua. And Santa Fe did have its pleasures, from dark-eyed ladies in lace mantillas to the humming gambling tables that operated alfresco on the central plaza night and day. For all its blemishes, the town, as a foreign capital, retained an exotic air and never quite lost its reputation as the chief lodestone in a land of promise.

Finally, William Becknell had started something else. The successful flow of caravan traffic, whose direction he had pointed, soon demonstrated the ease with which the United States might conquer the Southwest. His successors, without quite intending to do so, paved the way for the nation's expansion to the Pacific. Begun as an international highway of commerce, the Santa Fe Trail at the outbreak of the Mexican War in 1846 was transformed into the principal military road used by American forces bent on detaching the provinces of New Mexico and California from the Republic of Mexico. With the signing of a peace treaty two years later, providing for formal U.S. acquisition of invaded lands, the foot of the Santa Fe Trail was suddenly home territory, and the route itself took on new character as a domestic road. Until rails from the East reached Santa Fe in 1880, Becknell's old trail bore an ever-increasing tide of military freighters, mail couriers, stage passengers, and miners and emigrants bound for the far western goldfields. The man who had launched it all would live long enough to see how his little experiment back in 1821 had worked itself out.

William Becknell is buried neither in Franklin nor in Santa Fe, although each place would be honored to claim his mortal remains. He lies instead in an unkempt grave amid a copse of elm and hackberry trees just below the Red River in northeastern Texas. His biographer, Larry Beachum, took me there one steamy summer afternoon. The site is in the middle of a plowed field about five miles west of the town of Clarksville.

Becknell had come here in 1835 to get a fresh start, settling with his family, two slaves, and several of his old neighbors from the Boone's Lick country. Afterward he organized a volunteer company, called the Red River Blues, to fight in the Texas Revolution, and he served briefly in the congress of the Republic of Texas. The last two decades of his life (he died in 1856) were spent as a moderately prosperous farmer and stock raiser.

The setting of the neglected and unvisited grave seems to bear a special poignancy. Amid the poson ivy, Johnson grass, and snakes rests a man who carved a well-deserved niche for himself in the history books. Yet, in this lonely place I thought only of how fleeting are the ambitions and petty activities of us all. What little lasts beyond our own lifetime succumbs by stages to the obstinate erosion of time.

However, by hooking his star ever so briefly to the Santa Fe Trail, William Becknell seemingly earned an imperishable claim to immortality. Memory of the trail remains vigorously alive, and what imparts breath to that recollection are the uncommon experiences of people like Becknell who, over a period of three score years, wrote the story of that celebrated road stretching from Missouri westward to the smoke-colored mountains overhanging Santa Fe.

Although it may seem, from what I have related to this point, that the story of Old Franklin and the Boone's Lick country in the early 1820s revolved around the doings of William Becknell, that was far from the case. As a catalyst, he drove the wedge opening a new commerce in a new direction, but fairly quickly he withdrew from the scene and left the shaping of the Santa Fe trade to other men of the Missouri border who were better capitalized and perhaps more visionary.

These included such local luminaries as lawyer and politician John Heath, Benjamin Cooper and his nephew Stephen Cooper (members of a stalwart pioneer family), Franklin justice of the peace and postmaster Augustus Storrs, future governor of Missouri Meredith Miles Marmaduke, who kept a detailed diary of his 1824 journey to Santa Fe, and blue-eyed, black-haired Bailey Hardeman, younger brother of John Hardeman, whose Fruitage Farm the Missouri would wreck in 1826.

Prominent in Franklin also in those years was a pair of British-born brothers in their early twenties, David and William Workman. They operated a saddlery and harness shop, a prime business where caravans formed up for months of travel. In 1825 David, the junior of the two, abandoned steady employment at the workbench and joined what had now become the annual wagon train to Santa Fe. In so doing, he set a bad example for a teenage apprentice employed in the shop for the past year. Small, fair, and soft-spoken Christopher "Kit" Carson watched thoughtfully as William in his strange English accent bid brother David farewell.

Kit, one of ten children of Lindsey and Rebecca Carson, was born in Kentucky in 1809, the same year in which Abraham Lincoln and Charles Darwin were born. Soon afterward the Carsons, like generations of American families, migrated west, looking for land and a better life. They found both, or so it seemed, in the Boone's Lick country.

Lindsey Carson built a cabin for his brood and put in crops to feed them. When hostile Indians periodically ravaged the Missouri bottoms, he joined the militia to repel them. In one battle he engaged a warrior in hand-to-hand fighting, slaying his foe but losing two fingers in the bargain. All of his sons learned in childhood to handle a rifle and powder horn. In 1818 Lindsey was clearing a new field by burning off the timber when he was struck and killed by the limb of a falling tree.

The parents had intended that young Kit, who appeared to have a gift for learning, should one day be a lawyer. But after Lindsey's death that plan had to be abandoned. When Kit was fifteen, his mother apprenticed him to the Workmans to learn the saddler's trade.

By all accounts, the restless lad chafed at his confinement in the workshop. His older brothers had already entered the new West beyond the plains and the Rockies, becoming mountain men and traders. Two of them had gone to Santa Fe with a government survey party in 1825. Daily, the Workman's store in Franklin was crowded with men buying saddles, bridles, harnesses, and all the assorted leather rigging that was needed on the trail. Their talk of wild adventures and boundless opportunities that lay beyond the frontier was infectious. It inspired David Workman to make his parting, and it set the youthful Kit to plotting his own excape.

In late summer of 1826 he slipped away in the shank of the night and traveled several days by stealth along the rutted trace of the Santa Fe Trail until he found a wagon caravan that would hire him as a stock tender. In this way, the green lad began a career that would carry him into the history books and into the legends of a nation.

Although Kit Carson's subsequent exploits led from the Mexican border to the Canadian boundary and across the Sierra Nevada to the Pacific, the Santa Fe Trail time and again drew him back to its embrace. How many times he actually followed the trail in the course of his footloose life is difficult to say. But that it was one of the main keys to understanding his exceptional story cannot be doubted. Even as it played a major role in launching him on his life's work, so too did it take center stage at his passing. For Christopher Carson died in 1868 at Fort Lyon, Colorado Territory, square on the Mountain Branch of the Santa Fe Trail.

Anyone following the trail these days is never far from some marker or monument containing mention of Kit's own travels. Memorable incidents of his are recorded in all of the five trail states—Missouri, Kansas, Colorado, Oklahoma, and New Mexico. His career, as much as the old trail itself, after more than a century continues to bind those states in historical communion. And after all, walking in the footsteps of Kit Carson is part of the fascination to be discovered in retracing the grand and glorious road to Santa Fe.

So this, compressed in a thimble, is where and how it all began—at Franklin, bestride the majestic, brimming Missouri, with Becknell and Storrs, Marmaduke, the Carsons, the Workmans, Coopers, Hardemans, and a hallowed legion of others. Once the Santa Fe Trail was opened and the pattern set, its saga unfolded swiftly in a far-reaching and attenuated chain of interlocking events. One link led to the next, and so on, until 1880 when the railroad arrived in New Mexico and forever displaced the lowly ox train.

On that sweltering June day when I made my first pilgrimage to the head of the trail, I found on the main business street of New Franklin a tall monument dedicated to the exploits of William Becknell. I stood reading the message chiseled under a plaque cast in bronze relief which depicted his 1821 mule train in motion across the plains.

A middle-aged farmer in bib overalls wandered up, gave me a curious glance, and said: "Saw you standing thar lookin' at this thing. Ya know, I've lived in these parts all my life and I never took the trouble to find out what it says."

I smiled weakly, trying to hide my astonishment, and together we scanned the inscription. Under several lines acknowledging Becknell, appeared this:

FRANKLIN
"CRADLE OF THE SANTA FE TRAIL"
1821
THIS TRAIL
ONE OF THE GREAT HIGHWAYS OF THE WORLD
STRETCHED NEARLY ONE THOUSAND MILES FROM
FRANKLIN, MISSOURI TO SANTA FE, NEW MEXICO
FROM CIVILIZATION TO SUNDOWN

If ever the majesty of history was to be found in the written work, surely it resides in this simple but dramatic statement.

There in New Franklin on my initial visit I looked toward sundown, past green-robed bluffs to the bottomlands leading to the banks of the mighty Missouri River. And gazing beyond the dark waters, I imagined that I could see in sequence the primary trail landmarks studding the route all the way to Santa Fe. Their resonant names, as familiar to me as they were to the wagonmasters, conjured up images of rumbling wheels, rattling trace chains, and shouting teamsters.

Follow the Santa Fe Trail today past Franklin and you will still find them: Arrow Rock, Fort Osage, Independence and Westport Landing, Cave Spring, New Santa Fe (a village site on the Missouri-Kansas border), The Narrows, 110 Mile Creek, Council Grove, Lost Spring, Turkey Creek, Little Arkansas Crossing, Plum Buttes, Fort Zarah, Pawnee Rock, Fort Dodge, Cimarron Crossing, La Jornada, Willow Bar, The Rabbit Ears, Point of Rocks, El Vado de las Piedras, Wagon Mound, Fort Union, La Junta, San Miguel del Vado, Pecos Pueblo, Glorieta Pass, Rock Corral, and at last, rainbow's end, la Plaza de Santa Fe.

To me they were not lifeless place names sprinkled in an archipelago on yellowing, outdated maps. Rather, their listing pulses with a kind of mesmeric rhythm whose measured cadences entrance, while they draw you, through the use of informed imagination, into the misty chambers of the past. Why an old trail and its hoary landmarks should still possess the power to stir is a question I began to wrestle with the day I stood alongside the Franklin farmer. It was an enigma, I knew, that would haunt me until, somewhere down that thousand-mile road, I might with luck and perseverance stumble upon the answer.

In the days that followed, pursuing the trail on its own ground and in books and documents carried in my car, the pieces would gradually begin to come together. A mosaic comprising people, places, and events emerged and assumed intelligible shape. A sense of continuity took hold, of the unbroken progression of human activity from past to present. After a while I reached a point where my mind's eye started to see with greater clarity the entire panorama of the trail adventure. And with that new and sweeping view was born the recognition, ever so deeply felt, that yes!, each of us is indeed tied by a myriad of unseen threads to the yawning and silent gulf of the past. That which was here and alive before has retreated into history, by a process that will soon claim ourselves and what we now see around us.

Yet, the somberness of that reality, I would learn, is at least partially softened by the fact that some portion of the past always lingers to cojoin with the future: deeply grooved wagon tracks may be covered with the asphalt of an interstate highway, but it was spoked wheels that set the course now followed by speeding cars and trucks.

Out on the trail, crowded with reminders of that earlier day, vision seems to clear, our connection to yesterday becomes more apparent and the value of knowing where we have come from asserts itself like a self-evident imperative. When I first embarked upon the Santa Fe Trail, my understanding of that was dim, but after moving leisurely along the historic route the more important meanings slowly began to take hold. And in truth there lies the aim of all serious travel—to give the color of experience to our knowledge and to bring the hazy figures of our collective memory into sharper focus. In short, the winding trail, as I soon learned, is a place to experience the ineffable pleasure of discovery.

TWO

Independence and Westport

LONG BEFORE HE ASCENDED the golden stairs to the presidency, Harry S. Truman fancied himself a student of western trails. Being a lifelong resident of Independence, he came by that interest naturally. For his town, during a fleeting interval prior to the mid-nineteenth century, served as the starting gate at the head of the Santa Fe, Oregon, and California trails. Today walking the streets, as he often did on brisk winter mornings, one can sometimes catch the faint echo of those raw, noisy days when lively Independence was the bright star on America's frontier, and all those who had business in far western lands foregathered here to outfit, to make up their companies, and to take the fateful plunge into the prairie and mountain wilderness.

Just how strong was the president's commitment to trail lore can be seen at the Truman Library and Museum. Visitors innumerable go there to pay their respects to Harry and Bess, who rest in the open courtyard, and to view rooms of presidential memorabilia—his piano, china and paintings, a quaint 1940s limousine, less-than-edifying campaign buttons reading "Phooey on Dewey" and "I'm Just Wild About Harry." But the heart-stopper, covering an entire wall in the building's high-ceilinged lobby, is the massive Thomas Hart Benton mural entitled, *Independence and the Opening of the West.*

Just as he chose the theme, Truman also selected the painter, calling Benton "the best muralist in the country." During the eight months the work was in progress, the president watched closely and on occasion took brush in hand to add small blocks of solid color. When the mural was completed in 1961, it had caught, as perhaps no other piece of art has ever done, the vitality and spirit of trail life.

Native Missourian Benton was not only fitted by training and talent for the task, but he bore impeccable credentials by inheritance. He was grand-nephew and namesake of an earlier Thomas Hart Benton, one of Missouri's first senators after statehood and the unchallenged champion in Congress of federal support for the westward movement. Senator Benton, indeed, deserves much credit for helping to transform the helter-skelter Santa Fe trade, as it was in its early Franklin days, into the well-organized overland commerce that it became later in Independence.

The senator was firmly convinced that great empires were founded on trade and in that direction lay America's future strength. More to the immediate point, he saw advantage for his home state in nurturing the traffic Becknell had opened with Santa Fe. Already Mexican silver pesos were in wide use on the Missouri border, and the receiver of the Land Office in Franklin was accepting them from settlers in payment for government lands. When Franklin postmaster Augustus Storrs returned from Santa Fe late in 1824, Senator Benton sent him a list of questions concerning the character and needs of the Mexican trade. In his detailed response, Storrs provided the first authoritative view of this commerce. Benton had it printed as part of the congressional record early the following year.

Augustus Storrs ventured a couple of ideas on how the government might encourage this business that had sprung spontaneously from the efforts of private merchants. First he suggested that commissioners be appointed to survey the new trail to Santa Fe and mark it with mounds of earth to serve as guideposts. And second, he asked that American consuls be appointed for Santa Fe and Chihuahua, as he said, "to represent our interest and to negotiate concerning the duty on goods."

The following March, 1825, Senator Benton handily guided congressional passage of a bill for a survey of the Santa Fe Trail, with money tacked on to treat with Indians along the route for a right of way. At the same time, Augustus Storrs was named first U.S. consul to Santa Fe. Initiation of these measures gave official status to the trail and signified that the overland commerce was coming of age.

A new episode in the southwestward movement was ushered in later that year when a party of three commissioners, among whom George C. Sibley was the dominant member, set forth with a surveyor and assorted personnel for New Mexico. In the course of the two-year expedition, treaties were arranged with the Osage and Kansas Indians, the route was charted, earthen mounds called for by Storrs erected, and information about travel conditions collected. All of this is now of more interest to historians than it was originally of value to the

Sante Fe traders, because those resourceful traffickers were already accustomed to finding their own way and meeting head-on the challenges of prairie travel.

The Sibley survey, as it has come to be called, took its leave from Fort Osage, a pallisaded post perched on a seventy-foot bluff above the Missouri River and some ten miles east of the future site of Independence. It is there to this day, not the original walls and blockhouses, but a faithful reconstruction raised on the site in the 1960s. Built in 1808 by William Clark (of Lewis and Clark fame), Fort Osage was the last American outpost seen by Becknell and his men in 1821 on their pioneering trek to Santa Fe. George C. Sibley resided there as a government Indian trader in the years before he was named one of the road commissioners. Its place, therefore, in the history of the trail is firmly established.

Throughout the early and middle 1820s the line of settlement kept edging up the Missouri, beyond Franklin, as push-ahead pioneers sought fertile lands for farming. The town of Arrow Rock grew up on the river opposite Boone's Lick, and farther along the Osage Trace, Lexington blossomed as a frontier hamlet. Both places served briefly as outfitting points for Santa Fe–bound wagon trains. But it was Independence on the far side of the state, platted in 1827 and designated as seat of the newly created Jackson County, that was destined to gain command of the Mexican trade and win lasting renown as a trail head.

The fledgling town took root on a heavily wooded ridge, roughly midway between the Little Blue and Big Blue rivers, both of which emptied into the Missouri several miles north of Independence. It is said the streams drew their names from the clear blue water that washed their banks in those early days, a picture difficult to visualize now that they flow a drab olive green. Settlers called the surrounding lands the "Blue Country," whether after the rivers or from an autumnal haze, tinctured indigo, that colors the timbered slopes and bottoms, we cannot say. In any case, the picturesque landscape dotted with springs and furnished with a rich heavy soil attracted men of the plow well before men of commerce found in it a congenial locality for their own specialized activity.

In 1832 a touring Washington Irving pronounced Independence as existing upon "the utmost verge of civilization," and so indeed it must have seemed. Stumps of trees even then stippled the open ground on courthouse square. Rough log buildings lined the primitive dirt streets which became quagmires after heavy summer rains. At such times sturdy youths waded to church barefoot carrying Sunday shoes and socks in their hands and donning them at the door. And on all sides throughout the year the town was thronged with farmers, trappers in from the mountains, merchants, shopkeepers, and Indians of several tribes whose reservations lay eighteen miles to the west, across the Kansas line.

So, this was Independence as it began to grab the bulk of the Santa Fe trade from towns and villages farther east. With his Roman oratory and collar twisting in Congress, Senator Thomas Hart Benton had helped direct the events that led to its sudden rise to prominence. And, it was his descendant, bearing the same distinguished name, who managed to capture on wallspace at the Truman Library the spirit of Independence in its glory days.

I have spent several hours seated on a polished bench viewing Thomas Hart Benton's sweeping mural. Vast in scope, rich in authentic detail, it amply repays the time invested in careful study. However, I've noticed that it does have a tendency to overwhelm. Most visitors give it a casual glance, seeing but not seeing, and then pass on quickly to the presidential limousine and the glass cases with their campaign buttons. To appreciate fully what Benton has created, a person needs some knowledge of history, even more than an understanding of art. The mural pulses with the expansionist energy of the American West, but only an informed mind can assimilate it and draw meaning from it.

In all, Benton depicted more than forty people of different ages, occupations, and races who played some part on the trails that opened the West. There are Pawnee and Cheyenne Indians, French *voyageurs*, mountain men, hunters, explorers, early merchants (in the style of Becknell) with their packtrains of mules, and, of course, the inevitable pioneer family in its ox-drawn wagon, a popular image that epitomizes the emigrant road to Oregon. Two scenes in opposite corners are meant to symbolize the pair of trails that breathed life into Independence. In the upper right, a winding wagon train passes Chimney Rock in western Nebraska as it heads for Oregon, or perhaps for California, by following a branch trail angling down from Idaho. In the upper left corner rise the adobe ramparts of Bent's Fort, valued waystop on the pull to Santa Fe, and beyond the fort loom the snow-capped summits of the Spanish Peaks, landmarks admired by every southwestern traveler.

Artist Benton himself claimed that the people shown in his work represented generalized figures, each of whom was meant to stand for the type or class as a whole. Thus, one cannot identify Jim Bridger, whose career was closely tied to the Oregon Trail, or Kit Carson, a familiar fixture on the Santa Fe route. Instead, a single buckskin-clad plainsman toting a muzzleloader serves as a composite of all such men. Nevertheless, there appears to be at least one exception to Benton's self-imposed rule and that is in the depiction of Hiram Young, a free black whose Independence smithy and shop produced wagons as well as thousands of ox yokes, selling at a dollar and a quarter apiece to trail outfitters. Through diligence and thrift he eventually amassed an estate valued at more than $50,000, although much of it was lost during the turbulence of the Civil War.

The artist shows a lean and heavily muscled Hiram Young heating a piece of wagon iron in his forge, while a small, tow-headed boy pumps the bellows and an apprentice nearby shapes a horseshoe. Although Young, because of his race, was not typical of the many Independence businessmen who offered the variety of services required by overlanders, he does in the mural fittingly call attention to that vital function provided by the town.

By 1832 Independence had fully captured the Santa Fe trade, and a decade later, as the Oregon migration got under way, it truly became the gateway to the West. Even today, with nostalgic remembrance, the town speaks of itself as the "Queen City of the Trails." It earned its ranking because craftsmen, like Hiram Young, and storekeepers and livestock vendors and local farmers were all able to furnish a merchant or emigrant with the desired equipment and supplies. By purchasing wagons, oxen, mules, and foodstuffs here, rather than St. Louis or some intermediate point beyond that place, the traveler was able to cut his time on the road. More important, when he left Independence to brave the untamed West, he and his draft animals were fresh and the equipment spanking new.

Mainstay of the caravans was the huge freight wagon, often called a prairie schooner because in motion it resembled a heaving ship at sea. In paint, muralist Benton caught something of the majesty of this, the most typical of all western vehicles. The wagon bed was built higher in front and back with a slope toward the middle so that heavy loads on the mountain grades would shift to center. This distinctive shape added to its boatlike appearance. Hickory bows towered over the body forming arched supports for the white cover of Osnaburg canvas that repelled rain and resisted heat. When it became the custom to paint Santa Fe wagons a bright blue with red trim, the white tops completed a pleasing union of patriotic colors. Naturally after a few weeks on the trail, the canvas lost its brilliance and the paint its luster. Progressively, too, the wagon bodies began to look as if they had been attacked by beavers. On the high plains where timber was nonexistent and buffalo chips the only fuel, the teamsters in wet weather removed wooden shavings from the sides and tail gate to start their fires for coffee.

Eight mules or eight yoked oxen pulled the schooners. Mules cost more and were easily stampeded by Indians at night. But they traveled faster and could be ridden home if the merchant wished to sell his wagons in Santa Fe. Oxen were slow, but not only was their initial cost lower, they held up better on a steady diet of prairie grass. Since the wagons were filled to overflowing with merchandise, there was no room for riders. The mule skinner rode one of his lead mules. The bullwhacker, however, was obliged to walk beside his ox team the entire distance, unless his wagon happened to be fitted with a "lazy seat," a narrow board on the side that allowed him occasionally to take his ease. The whacker's badge of office was a twenty-foot whip which he could pop with the sound of a Fourth of July firecracker.

The Santa Fe traders, who supervised the caravan's march, rode sleek saddle mules. Dressed in linsey-woolsey shirts, broadcloth trousers, frock coats, and black felt hats, they took the point position to scan the road ahead for trouble but also to avoid the lung-stinging dust churned up by the mighty wagon wheels. At the forming up for the initial departure from Independence Square, the traders moved briskly through the noise and confusion produced by bawling teamsters and resisting animals new to the harness or yoke. Upon the bedlam they imposed order so that finally with the cry of "All's set!" the cavalcade lurched forward amid the cheers of bystanders, and another journey to Santa Fe was under way.

Strolling around the present-day square, serene and modern, one scarcely gets a hint of the stir history once made here. I was fortunate on my first visit to be given an introduction by local archivist Polly Fowler. As we walked the perimeter, she pointed out the sites where the buildings known to the Santa Fe traders had once stood. Only one original structure remained, the three-story Nebraska House, a celebrated hostelry whose guest book bore names that loomed large in the story of the West. When I returned a year later, the Nebraska House had been demolished and an asphalt parking lot occupied its place.

Between Independence and Santa Fe can still be found a fair number of buildings, monuments, and landmarks left over from the era of the trail. But in almost every case, it can be shown that some individual or group fought heroically, and often against formidable odds, to save them. That is true even of the attractive and significant courthouse that practically fills Independence Square. It postdates the covered-wagon period, but it was built upon part of the original walls and basement of the smaller red brick courthouse that greeted overlanders headed for New Mexico and Oregon. In 1970 plans were afoot to raze the structure. A band of iron-muscled preservationists, however, took up the gauntlet with determination, and their foes soon yielded. The task was eased by the fact that the building contained the office and the courtroom where County Judge Harry S. Truman had once presided.

Nevertheless, the square now looks nothing like the one sketched in 1845 by a local artist, showing handsome blocks of stores and residences and a crowd of wagons, horsemen, and gawking townsfolk. Because Polly Fowler and I knew something of our history we were able, by the exercise of creative imagination, to reconstruct a picture of this place in a time long gone and to resurrect momentarily the sounds, smells, and feel that once were part of its unique character. Lacking any knowledge of the past, the average person, I suppose, will see Courthouse Square as flat, one-dimensional, and stuck in the present, or near-present. That is a view with all of the life and vitality squeezed from it, and one that promotes the notion that history is irrelevant.

Therein would seem to lie the larger importance of Thomas Hart Benton's mural at the nearby Truman Library. His sprawling *Independence and the Opening of the West* jerks us out of the present. It opens the mind to the reality of western spaciousness. It forces upon us the difficult realization that men and women walked before us in full sunlight, that we are the products of their experience and effort, and that we belong, conscious of it or not, to a human flow that reaches backward at the same instant it is ebbing forward. All along the Santa

Fe Trail, elements of that message manifest themselves, lending substance and purpose to a modern retracing of the route. So, while any authentic start must be made at the head-of-the-trail marker in Franklin, the spiritual or philosophical beginning of any trip, I like to think, must take place in front of the Benton mural.

One last thing about that painting: in the lower left, where the eye must search it out, is a steamboat moored at one of Independence's two river landings several miles north of town. Shuttle wagons are drawn up to receive the cargo which will be transferred to Courthouse Square or to campgrounds just beyond for loading on the larger Santa Fe wagons. It was the development and improvement of steam navigation, in the years just after Independence's founding, that boosted the town toward supremacy as a trail head.

The Missouri River, broadest of the Mississippi's fifty-nine navigable tributaries, was well situated to serve as a main avenue to the Great West. Near its mouth on the east was St. Louis, whose wharves and ramshackle warehouses overflowed with the goods required by Indian traders, fur traders, and Santa Fe traders. Slicing directly across the state past Franklin, Arrow Rock, Fort Osage, Independence, and the future site of Kansas City, the Missouri finally bent northwest toward Nebraska and its eventual headwaters on the eastern slope of the Continental Divide.

Early on, upriver traffic was by keelboat which used a combination of sails, oars, and cordelling (men walking the shore and hauling by ropes) to force a passage against the powerful current. But then in May 1819, the first steamboat ascended the Missouri to Franklin where residents cheered its arrival and feted its officers with as lavish a dinner as the frontier allowed. Two more steamers appeared a few weeks later; one of them, the *Western Engineer,* had a large figure of a serpent projecting from its bow. From the open mouth a pipe emitted clouds of steam from the engines. More smoke and streams of sparks rose out of the chimney. Indians who chanced to see this fiendish apparition from the shore fled in terror while the crew on board roared with laughter.

At the outset Independence was established strictly as a farming community back from the river, with little thought given to the fact that it might soon emerge as a commercial center. In any case, high cliffs lifting precipitously from the water's edge and breaking behind into low hills precluded placement of the town much closer to the Missouri. Below, other towns on the right bank like Lexington, Arrow Rock, and Booneville, also had to contend with steep bluffs walling them off from the river. But at each place a spit of land along the shoreline gave room for a boat landing accessible by a road carved out of the heights.

The first Missouri steamboats were slow and clumsy with blunt bows making them worse than washtubs to steer. But by the 1830s new designs in structure and rearrangement of furnaces and boilers improved speed and handling. The old keelboats had needed a month to inch their way from St. Louis upstream to Independence. But now that time was cut by more than two-thirds, so that goods awaited by trail outfitters reached them with unheard of dispatch.

So the steamboats came, paddling against the current with a flurry of bell-ringing, the stern-wheelers and side-wheelers thrashing the waters of the Big Muddy into green spray. The tall stacks poured forth clouds of villainous smoke and showered the wooden decks with glowing sparks that sometimes set the boat on fire and burned it to water level. High up in the pilothouse the man at the wheel kept a sharp lookout for sandbars and the treacherous snags that lurked just below the surface. On the decks passengers crowded the rails watching, as each bend was rounded, for first sight of the next landing.

One afternoon Polly Fowler and I took an excursion on a large motorized flatboat which, although failing to duplicate precisely the old-time steamboat, at least gave us a sense of what river travel was all about. The current in the main channel sweeps on and on with its original, undiminished vigor. The savage sandbars and snags are still there. The shores in many places remain thickly grown with elm, willows, hickory, honey locust, laurel bush, and woodbine and liberally festooned with flood debris. Even where enormous bridges span the river and tall buildings can be seen inland, you get the impression from this view that the Missouri somehow belongs more to the past than to the present.

At Independence Landing, the steamboats from St. Louis docked and were quickly pushed slantwise by the current. Gangplanks were swung into place and black stevedores, singing in chorus, began off-loading all the merchandise marked for Santa Fe and Chihuahua. That not immediately put into the shuttle wagons was stowed on the wharf under heavy canvas tarps and left unguarded overnight, for, strange to tell, no one seemed inclined to pilfer. Observing all this activity with silent interest were weather-battered men in greasy buckskins, recently arrived from the western wilderness, who lounged on the landing and nipped at jugs of tanglefoot whiskey. The hubbub and color of the scene provided a fitting prelude for the larger drama that was to follow—the two-month journey across prairie and mountain to the final act played out on the Santa Fe plaza.

But as the river giveth, so can the river taketh away. Scarcely had Independence established its commercial dominance when an upstart rival appeared a dozen miles farther west, near the Kansas line. Westport came to life as a log-cabin hamlet in 1835 when storekeeper John McCoy, son of a Baptist missionary to the Indians, began subdividing land adjacent to his place of business. The location was ideal—four miles south of the Missouri River and adjacent to open prairie offering natural pastureland. Just across the state boundary was then Indian Territory, containing reserves for defeated tribes displaced from the East. Receiving annuities from the government they had money to spend and, until Westport appeared, no place handy to spend it. Other stores grew up rapidly alongside McCoy's, as well as taverns, the one built by Daniel Yoacham being the first. "Westport," said one visitor, "was full of Indians whose shaggy ponies were tied by the dozens along the houses and fences." And he noted that whiskey circulated more freely than was altogether safe in a place where every man carried a loaded pistol in his pocket.

By the early 1840s men involved in the Santa Fe trade began to notice that Westport had matured from a wide place in the road to a fair-size town capable of providing services and supplies to overlanders. A wagon road led north to the river where a fine stone shelf of a landing offered easy access to the water. Boat pilots were especially pleased because the Missouri here was free of the troublesome sandbars that plagued the two landings at Independence. Moreover, the bluffs were much diminished at this point so that wheeled vehicles had an easier time making the grade out of the bottoms.

And, Westport had other features to recommend it. For one, its situation at the very edge of the advancing frontier meant that caravans making up here, rather than at Independence, saved a dozen miles of travel. They also avoided having to cross the Big Blue River lying midway between the two towns. Its steep banks were always an unpleasant hurdle for wagons, and during the spring freshet high water often made fording impossible, occasioning serious and expensive delays. Further, as Independence grew and new population filled in the outlying tracts, that community became less able to accommodate large wagon trains. Open pasturage, available to huge herds of draft stock, shrunk, and farmers increasingly fenced off the public road that formerly had meandered through vacant lands.

All these factors combined gradually to pull trail business away from Independence and to deliver it by the late 1840s firmly into the hands of Westport. The conveniences offered by the latter had won over the Santa Fe traders. William R. Bernard, head of one of the newly prosperous mercantile houses, recalled long afterward that in the springtime, "The prairies south of the town . . . were covered with tents and wagons and appeared like the camp of a great army." That army swelled prodigiously when, at the end of the decade, ranks of '49ers, off for the California goldfields, took their place in the teeming campgrounds. Altogether, the miners, Oregon emigrants, and Santa Fe traders are said to have assembled 40,000 trail vehicles at Westport in the years 1849 and 1850.

It was in the 1850s that the town reached the zenith of its prosperity associated with trail business. In the banner year of 1857, some 300 traders and freighters, engaged in New Mexican commerce, paid out $1.5 million to Westport merchants, blacksmiths and wheelwrights, livestock producers, and bullwhackers. That year a record 729 boats found berth at Westport Landing and disgorged mountains of crates, boxes, trunks, barrels, and hogsheads to be piled upon the wharf. By then steamboats had become glamour craft embellished with gingerbread scroll and fancy ironwork, the interiors of the upper cabins richly carpeted and hung with dazzling glass chandeliers. Steam travel on the Missouri and the town of Westport had come of age together.

They also accompanied one another in decline during and immediately after the Civil War. The advent of hostilities quickly crippled Westport's complex web of commercial activity, disrupted the passage of traffic to and from Santa Fe, and brought a partial halt to the armada of steamers plying the Missouri River. Western Missouri and eastern Kansas dissolved into a bloody battleground between southern bushwhackers and northern jayhawkers, merciless guerrillas all. In Westport people hungered, lived in stables when their homes were torched, and some women and children saw their menfolk dragged into the street and shot before their eyes. The road eastward across the Big Blue to Independence was marred by smoldering farmhouses and blackened fields.

During the war years, what small part of the Santa Fe trade did not completely lapse moved up the Missouri twenty miles to Fort Leavenworth (founded in 1827) where the federal garrison provided a measure of protection. But with peace in 1865, the surviving merchants returned to Westport and to Westport Landing, around whose warehouses just above dockside a respectable community was already in evidence. In fact, even before the war the landing settlement was being called Kansas City with the anticipation that it would one day expand to assume metropolitan dimensions. It did that, of course, even before the century was out, stretching its limits south to engulf its fading parent community, Westport, in 1897. With the sudden explosion of railroad building in the wake of the Civil War, track had swiftly been laid into eastern Kansas. Westport thereby lost its role as a trail center, just as Franklin and Independence before it had succumbed. Simultaneously the popularity and usefulness of river traffic waned, as the steamboat made way for the train.

However, all of this was in the distant future for what may be reckoned as the palmy days of the Santa Fe Trail—the period from about 1832 to mid-century when the march of the prairie schooners was in its most exuberant phase and Independence and Westport were vying for supremacy. Out of those years come some of our best trail chronicles giving us the stories and the images that characterize the heyday of the southwestern trade. And within that era as well can be found the most spirited and colorful participants in that enterprise.

The Santa Fe Trail emerged as a road unlike any other in America's westward movement. As a thoroughfare founded on international commerce, it showed few similarities to the Oregon, California, and Mormon emigrant roads and practically none to the later cattle trails that assumed such a large role in our national folklore. In microcosm one can encounter in the Santa Fe Trail experience almost all of the elements that forged the distinctive American character and ethic. Risk-taking, unbridled optimism, a certain level of disregard for personal comfort and safety, self-confidence, individual initiative and inventiveness, an exaggerated notion of the superiority of one's own customs and culture, and a corresponding disdain for the ways of other people (in this case Indians and Mexicans), extraordinary mental resiliency and physical adaptability, and above everything else a single-minded devotion to the quest for profit in the market-place—all of these figured in the mix to a high degree. In sum, a trip to Santa Fe was an adventure into the very heart of what America was all about.

THREE

To Council Grove and the Great Beyond

IN HIS BEST-SELLING TRAVEL BOOK *Blue Highways*, author William Least Heat Moon proclaims that the true beginning of the West is marked by an almost straight line running north to south that forms the western boundaries of Louisiana, Arkansas, Missouri, Iowa, and Minnesota. "Stand on one side of that line," he advises, "and you are in the East. Cross over and you have arrived in the West." There is a large dose of truth in his statement, as the Santa Fe traders would have been the first to attest.

As the freight wagons rolled out of Westport, they crossed the border from Missouri into Kansas almost before the mules had fully settled into the harness. At once the air changed and the land took on a different aspect, a fact duly noted by those traders keeping journals. From Franklin to this point, the Missouri countryside had been a mixture of open prairie and woodland, a combination much favored by pioneer settlers. But from the moment one passed into Kansas, the dense stands of timber melted away, and the ever-widening grasslands took command. Only along creeks and rivulets and in small hollows could woody growth be found—oak, hickory, dogwood, and willow springing from thickets of hazel bushes. As the Santa Fe trade progressed, thousands of travelers scavenging for firewood took a heavy toll on the sparse trees close to the trail.

Another change in the landscape was also noticeable. Large, deep rivers offering impediments to wagon traffic virtually disappeared. The last one was the Big Blue, a few miles past Independence. As we mentioned, Westport's ascendency was owing in part to its location west of that barrier. Westport merchant William R. Bernard tells us that from the Kansas boundary, "the trail was free from any stream of magnitude for a distance of at least eighty miles, or to the present site of Burlingame, Kansas." The water there was called Switzler Creek, named for John Switzler who spanned it with a toll bridge in 1847. But even before addition of that convenience, wagons had little trouble in making the shallow ford. Back in 1824, Augustus Storrs had informed Senator Benton that one of the sterling merits of the Santa Fe Trail was that it lay open, level, and free from hindrances to the base of the Rocky Mountains. Others agreed, adding the observation that no other route of comparable length across the continent could be so easily traversed by wagons. It was mainly the absence of broad and swift rivers, of the kind bedeviling the Oregon pioneers, that elicited these enthusiastic recommendations.

Whether leaving from Independence or Westport, one got the feeling almost immediately of entering a new and different environment, wild and as yet untouched by the softening hand of civilization. As he rode by the last outlying farmhouse southwest of Independence in 1839, Matt Field turned in the saddle to see "the solitary christian roof fade rapidly down to the horizon's verge, as the desert opens still vaster and wilder in advance." "Here it is," affirms writer William Least Heat Moon, speaking from a contemporary perspective, "that the true West differs from the East in one great, pervasive, influential, and awesome way: space." It is that spaciousness, the sense of airiness and unlimited distance, which impressed itself upon Field, that forced change upon man's activity, institutions, outlook, and manner of thinking. To the degree that he adapted and responded to the new challenge, the Santa Fe traveler experienced a metamorphosis—the easterner shed his coat and became a westerner. In the process, his view of the world, heretofore pinched by a narrow southern or midwestern upbringing, expanded enormously.

Kansas City and its satellite communities have now sprawled across square miles by the score so that when driving the interstate highway alongside the old Santa Fe trace, it is practically impossible to get that feeling of roominess spoken of by the wagoners. For me, not until I clear the booming little city of Olathe and enter upon narrow and thinly traveled U.S. 56 (usually called the Santa Fe Trail Highway), do I sense that the crowded East has been left behind. My reward is in the thought that at the end of the far-flung space unfolding ahead lies Santa Fe and home, nestled in the mountains of New Mexico.

About eight miles down the highway from Olathe and just past the little town of Gardner, modern drivers come to a historic fork in the road. In trail days, one fork turned right aiming more than two thousand miles for Oregon. The other, veering left, continued on to Santa Fe. The German naturalist Adolphus Wislizenus reached the junction in 1846 and saw a crude signpost there reading "Road to Oregon." And he suggested, "to Japan, China, and the East Indies, might have been added." In the center of the Y today is a Kansas Historical Society marker commemorating the parting of two of America's most celebrated trails. The old Oregon route is a gravel farm road at present, while the road to Santa Fe has become a trim ribbon of asphalt leading toward Council Grove, another hundred miles down the way.

Reference has been made to the narrow zone along the western edge of Missouri where the woods that begin on the Atlantic coast finally surrender to the open prairie and where the Santa Fe freighters initially sensed that their familiar world had been left behind. On the long road to New Mexico, they would encounter other lines, less distinct perhaps, but all representing a transition to circumstances and conditions not previously encountered. The next such line was met along the sparkling little Neosho River, at the prairie Eden called Council Grove.

The significance of the place was severalfold. Foremost was its choice location, forming one of the most agreeable stops anywhere on the trail. An abundance of water, wood, and grass—the three requisites for a perfect campsite—prompted caravans to pause for rest and repair. With the first and easiest leg of the trip done, it was time for a shakedown and a tightening up of equipment. It was a good place also to look ahead in anticipation of problems that awaited. To that end, and here lies the second reason for Council Grove's importance, the teamsters went busily to work felling trees and fashioning spare wagon tongues and axle trees to be stowed away under the vehicles. Clustered on both banks of the Neosho for a mile or more were oak, hickory, walnut, and ash, laced with grapevines thick as a man's wrist, the last large stand of hardwoods on the trail west. Under one spectacular and sprawling oak, close to the ford, Sibley and the other trail commissioners in 1825 had joined in solemn council with the Osage and hammered out the treaty providing secure passage for the caravans. From that landmark incident, the site took its name.

A third matter of consequence was that travelers recognized Council Grove as the gateway to hostile Indian country. The farther they got beyond the Neosho and the lands of the relatively peaceful Osage and Kaw tribes, the deeper they penetrated the raiding territory of predatory Pawnee, Apache, Kiowa, and Comanche. Therefore, from Council Grove forward, night guards were posted and the wagons were drawn into a hollow square or a rough circle for protection.

Since safety was not an issue to this point, caravans often left the Missouri border piecemeal, moving out in segments as they were ready and halting at Council Grove, where pasture on adjacent prairies was unlimited, to wait arrival of the rest of the train. The site thus became the out-trail rendezvous for the entire Santa Fe trade, and in the eyes of some of the participants the actual launching ground for any journey to New Mexico. On the basis of that, the present town fathers of Council Grove have posted signs on the outskirts proclaiming it the "Birthplace of the Santa Fe Trail."

As the Indian danger ahead became more acute with the passing years, necessity forced the traders to band together in larger and larger trains. Some of those that assembled at Council Grove were composed of a hundred wagons or more, plus Dearborn carriages bearing health seekers or other individual travelers and even a cannon or two. The entire convoy, when stretched out, might reach a mile. Since every man toted a rifle, the strongest war parties tended to think twice before committing mischief.

Management of the convoy, or the "annual caravan" as it was popularly known, could not be left to chance. When all had gathered in the thick shade of the hardwood grove, it fell to every man to elect a captain of the train. Occasionally, there was an obvious candidate upon whom all could agree, as happened whenever Charles Bent was present. He was the senior partner of the mercantile firm Bent, St. Vrain & Company, builders of Bent's Fort on the upper Arkansas, and an individual well schooled in plainscraft. But usually, the American penchant for politics asserted itself, and the camp broke into partisan factions, each election-eering furiously on behalf of its man. "A great deal of bickering and wordy warfare" is how one trader describes it. Bitterness remaining from such campaigns some-times resurfaced during moments of crises down the road.

On the whole, however, the captain's orders were scrupulously complied with. Members of the caravan, being solid frontier types, exhibited a resolute inde-pendence, but that trait, as a potential source of trouble, was largely offset by another quality, already firmly rooted in our national character: a willingness to conform to the rules of the democratic process. The captain, then, as spokesman for the governed, apportioned the caravan into divisions (each under a lieu-tenant), made assignments for guard duty, named the pilot (as the guide or scout was then termed), and determined the schedule for the day's march. It was a system that, once institutionalized, worked uncommonly well.

All of these little details are never far out of mind when I come to Council Grove. It was a special place for wagon travelers and it remains a special place for me. A tranquil community of 2,600 people and one short commercial street, far off both the Kansas Turnpike and Interstate 70, it presents a storybook picture of small-town America. What lifts it out of the ordinary and lends distinction is that old trail whose presence, even after all these years, continues to make itself felt. There is scarcely a block that is not graced with some marker or historical sign. And most any citizen, met while wandering the streets, can provide you a capsule history of the days when traders were thickly camped along the Neosho.

My meal headquarters in Council Grove is the two-story Hays House Restau-rant, a half block beyond the river ford. It claims, with ample justification, to be the oldest eating establishment west of the Mississippi. The builder in 1857 was Seth Hays, a great-grandson of Daniel Boone and a cousin of Kit Carson. His tavern and hostelry—now the restaurant— served wayfarers on the Santa

Fe route as well as local folks, for by that date a village had sprung up trailside. First, during the Mexican War, the army had built a wagon repair depot. Then, the firm of Waldo, Hall & Company opened a stage station, shops, and corrals to serve its Santa Fe coaches. The same year that Seth Hays put up his tavern, merchant Tom Hill constructed a small limestone building on the west side of town and called it "The Last Chance Store." He advertised it as: "The last chance to buy supplies between Council Grove and Santa Fe." Except for his little store, which still stands, Tom Hill would be long forgotten.

I like a window table at the Hays House because it allows me to look upon the road where fleets of wagons wearing white canvas bonnets once passed. Munching on one of the house specialties, marinated beef brisket or home-fried chicken, seems to bring the diner closer somehow to that lost era. And if a person is lucky enough to have the restaurant's genial hosts give a tour of the building from top story to basement, he will find opportunities to rub hands on original stonework and hand-adzed beams set in place by Seth Hays himself.

In the accumulation of such small experiences, I think the modern individual can begin to grasp the authentic character of the Santa Fe Trail. Pulling facts from books and building up images of trail life drawn from first-hand journals is necessary, without doubt. But to reach a more fundamental level of understanding, raw data must be combined with one's own on-the-scene experiences and observations. Through a mysterious process of mental alchemy, the remote and seemingly lifeless past suddenly appears suffused with new light. Men and women long dead walk the trail again. Oxen lean into their yokes. Dogs silent for a century bark once more. And the mists of mornings gone creep silently down from the Flint Hills behind Council Grove to fill the timbered bottoms bracketing the lazy curves of the Neosho. At such times the mind can clear for an instant, as if the congestion of a head cold has suddenly drained away, and vision stretches backward, momentarily granting that long view I've spoken of before—the one that lets us see history's sweep and our own place in the unfolding scheme of things. That experience, once tasted, becomes addictive.

In these intensely personal encounters with the past, my greatest pleasure derives from intimate acquaintance with the makers of history. People, who recorded in trail diaries not only the lively details of their adventuring, but also something of their innermost thoughts, often reveal more of themselves to readers than they did to family and associates who knew them personally. Getting to know them in this way allows you to form a one-way friendship across the barrier of time. Among the most accessible of such individuals, and the one toward whom my thoughts inevitably turn when in Council Grove, is Josiah Gregg. He it was who perhaps epitomizes best the essence, the zest, the excitement, and the full sum of the Santa Fe Trail.

Gregg is remembered as the chief chronicler of the trail whose two-volume

Commerce of the Prairies, published in 1844, overnight became the Bible for all those contemplating entry into the Santa Fe trade. But when he first saw Council Grove in the spring of 1831, on the first of his four trips to Santa Fe and four trips back, he was a rank greenhorn. Then twenty-five years of age, Josiah Gregg was handsome as a picture, with a firm jaw and a high forehead bespeaking superior intelligence. Unfortunately, he was also much debilitated by ill health, virtually an invalid according to his own declaration.

Son of a wheelwright who migrated from Tennessee to Illinois and finally to Independence, Josiah had two strikes against him as a child of the frontier—that sickly constitution which rendered him unfit for heavy labor and an avid liking for books fueled by his scholarly thirst for knowledge. His education, encouraged by a sensitive mother, was largely self-acquired. As a youth he mastered Latin, French, Italian, and German; studied surveying; and read law, with the intention of becoming an attorney. But all thoughts of earning a livelihood were soon pushed in the shade by what he diagnosed as the "morbid condition of my system which originated in the familiar miseries of dyspepsia and its kindred infirmities." What he was saying is that his multiple afflictions baffled the medical men of the day.

They had, however, one last, desperate remedy to offer. As Gregg himself tells it: "In my hopeless condition, the physicians advised me to take a trip across the prairies, and in the change of air and habits which such an adventure would involve to seek that health which their science had failed to bestow. I accepted their suggestion . . . joining one of the spring caravans starting from the United States for Santa Fe."

The prescription worked! When his friends bid farewell in Independence, Josiah Gregg lay flat on his back in a wagon, scarcely able to move. But within a week he was up and walking and by the time Council Grove was reached, he could mount a horse. Beyond the Neosho, with the sighting of the first scattered buffalo, the patient who had recently appeared on the brink of death, eagerly joined in the chase. Gregg's biographer, Paul Horgan, suggests that "it was life on the trail which brought his energies alive again."

If that guess is accurate, as it seems to be, we may here perhaps find vindication of an old notion, recently brought down from the attic and polished up by today's so-called wellness movement—the idea that cures can often be effected when the doctors withdraw and leave the ailing body to restore itself using its own vast recuperative powers. But Horgan's observation really advances something more, for note that "life on the trail" became the catalyst that turned the body from infirmity toward robustness.

Gregg, quite unintentionally, provides us a further insight. He writes: "The effects of this journey were in the first place to re-establish my health, and, in the second, to begat a passion for prairie life which I never expect to survive."

He seems to think that his recovery and his new passion were separate and distinct, whereas in fact his sudden devotion to a newly discovered, stimulating way of life in all probability triggered the physiological mechanisms needed for a return to soundness. Challenge, a change of scene, discovery, the element of danger, and hardships that heighten the sense of awareness, acting individually or in concert, can recharge a lethargic will and grant a cleansed view of endless possibilities in living, previously overlooked.

In this, and especially in his reference to "a passion for prairie life," Josiah Gregg leads us closer to an explanation of the deeper meaning underlying the entire Santa Fe Trail experience. For what, we may ask, were the elements exerting their appeal that led so many people, like Gregg, to acquire an overwhelming yen for the trail? George D. Brewerton contributes to an answer when upon arriving in Independence from Santa Fe in 1848 he said of his travels, "We enjoyed high physical health and wonderful appetites, and withal a feeling of self-reliance, which inspired us with a consciousness of superior power; for we had breathed the pure atmosphere of the Great Prairies until every nerve was braced, and every sinew was strengthened to its fullest vigor." That glad-to-be-alive feeling swelled in the chest as a person moved across the spacious grasslands and partook of the quintessental freedom that was the American West's most precious gift. Brewerton saw that, and articulated it as did others.

Josiah Gregg spoke of the "high excitement which attached him so strongly to prairie life," and when, after nine years as a Santa Fe trader, he retired to compose his *Commerce of the Prairies* and then pursue a career in medicine, he wrote nostalgically, "Scarcely a day passes without my experiencing a pang of regret that I am not now roving at large upon those western plains." After regaining his health on the first trip, during which time he mastered the mechanics of the trade, he had become a merchantman and gone on to accumulate considerable financial success. But profit aside, he makes clear that he regarded his western wayfaring as a splendid lark.

Precisely how much of the same motive animated other Santa Fe traders is a bit difficult to say, but that it figured in all of them to some degree seems an inescapable conclusion. Businessmen with loaded wagons hoped for safe passage across the prairies and through Indian country and, in the end, for a profitable trade at Santa Fe. Nevertheless, they were intrigued by the unpredictability of the trip and the chances it offered to use their wits in overcoming the dangerous and stormy forces that lay along the way. On the trail the even tenor of life in towns was exchanged for regular draughts of high adventure, so that a fellow moved through the day with attention focused, senses alert, and an acute and constant recognition of his own mortality. He knew he was alive!

In time the Santa Fe traders, those who remained in the game, became finely tuned to the rhythm of the trail. Yearly passage back and forth on the same route soon made them familiar with each campsite and landmark and that familiarity bred fondness. Franz Huning, a German immigrant who joined the trade as a youth in the 1850s, told his grandson in the early twentieth century that he had known each designated stopping place on the Santa Fe Trail as well as he knew his own living room and that at every one he had felt comfortable and at home. He was not unique in that sentiment.

Through regular crossings of the prairie, the traveler soon learned the lore of the trail, the small histories connected with each camp and landmark. Niko Tinbergen, though far removed from the Southwest, could just as well have been speaking of the Santa Fe overlanders when he wrote in *Curious Naturalists:* "We lived in that country long enough to have seen it in a great variety of circumstances and moods, and gradually every part of it acquired significance; the whole area became charted with our experiences, many of which I shall never forget."

Here we see a major departure from the situation on the Oregon Trail. For most of the farming folk bound for the Pacific Northwest theirs was a one-way journey, and usually a nightmarish one at that. Those who survived the multiple perils of the trail scarcely ever looked back upon the overland experience as something they would want to repeat. They lacked both the opportunity to gain familiarity with the route and the desire to do so. Among them ripened no affinity for life in the wilds as it did among the Missouri traders.

Surely, if we believe the written accounts of participants, part of the allure of the Santa Fe Trail was to be found in the natural beauty of the prairie and mountain landscape. To the uninitiated the enormity of western spaces could seem intimidating, frightening. But to veteran travelers grown accustomed to far-reaching horizons, the journey became, according to one, "a dream of picturesque and never-to-be-forgotten pleasure." And, wrote another: "The air . . . is many times clearer and incomparably drier than in the eastern part of the United States, and the heavens burn nightly with millions of magnified stars which the people of the East never dreamed of." The wide land and shifting viewscapes, the air, the night sky's dome spangled with stars provided a bonus, or better said, compensation for the routine trials and sufferings that accompanied any ride to Santa Fe.

While excitement, challenge, and awe-inspiring scenery furnished the ingredients for the trail's special magnetism and fed Gregg's "passion for prairie life," there is, of course, more to the story. Without the strong mercantile impulse and the willingness of frontier merchants to risk their small accumulations of capital in a foreign market, there would have been no Santa Fe Trail, at least in the beginning. During those years, in the decades before the mid-nineteenth century, America was a land mainly of farmers and merchants, and it was among the latter that you found men of ambition and superior learning. "Our national virtues are the virtues of merchants . . . ," proclaimed the *American Review* in 1845.

In hustling to turn a buck, the frontier trader learned the best techniques for moving bolts of cloth, hardware, cutlery, clothing, and a dozen other categories of goods from east to west over vast distances. He became adept at collaborating with others and in meeting competitors head on. He mastered the Spanish language. (Gregg did on his initial trip, studying a grammar and conversing with several Mexican teamsters.) He perfected his negotiating abilities with Indians of the plains and with customs officials at Santa Fe. In short the trader honed his skill at solving concrete problems. That skill, when combined with a ready willingness to face challenges, nourished the towering self-confidence and "consciousness of superior power" spoken of by George Brewerton.

I think it helps to remember everything said thus far regarding the character and motives of the early traders, because in wandering modern-day Council Grove you get a sense of their presence and begin to realize that we are dealing here with an extraordinary group of people. Complex in their personalities, serious of purpose, and imbued with courage to a high degree, they boldly and willingly crossed the Neosho to continue a march filled with uncertainties. Since we are the products of an indulgent society, far less fitted for elemental struggles than were these pioneer merchants, we can't help but find something instructive in reflecting upon their daring.

For a wider view of Council Grove than the one offered by a window seat in the Hays House, I drove up on an elevation east of town, about a half mile from the river. Near the Hilltop Cafe is a grassy overlook and one of the Daughters of the American Revolution granite trail markers. I believe it was here that some of the wagons began camping in the 1850s after Seth Hays and others had preempted the land around the ford to lay the start for a community. Gazing across rooftops to the rising plain beyond, I tried to picture Josiah Gregg's caravan in motion and to imagine what was in his head, particularly on that maiden trip when he submitted his disease-weakened body to the stern demands of the trail. My speculations may not have summoned his exact thoughts, but probably they gave me some fair inkling of his frame of mind. In the process I caught a fleeting sensation of what it was actually like to breach the Neosho and be propelled upon the wide arc of the prairie ocean where the tall grass rippled to the touch of the wind and the land stretched empty, seemingly on forever.

The emptiness, that phenomenon of unrelieved spaciousness of which we made pointed mention at the opening of this chapter, was, of course, more apparent than real. By Gregg's day the Santa Fe Trail was plainly marked by wagon tracks deeply scored in the earth. And along its entire length were the named campsites, most with some source of water, known to every pilot and caravan captain. Indeed, any person who made as much as a single crossing came away with a map firmly fixed in his memory of the trail and its detours, camps, fords, and natural landmarks. He also brought knowledge of the roving tribes apt to be met in the course of a journey. As a result, those travelers who were seasoned hands saw the sprawling country not as vacant wasteland but as a boundless place containing much that was interesting and challenging.

In the course of my comings and goings, west from Council Grove, I have formed my own mental map of the trail as it exists today. Most of the historic points, listed by Gregg in his itinerary, find room upon it. Around each clusters the memory of long-ago incidents representative of the humorous, the heroic, the tragic, and the ennobling aspects of trail experience. For those who follow today's highway to Santa Fe, the journey takes on the character of a pilgrimage through the past, when those incidents are recalled and their significance pondered while standing on the very ground where they happened. Dedicated trail buffs who get caught up in such business soon discover that they have collected their own stock of firsthand experiences—a flat tire here, a storm encountered there, unusual or trailwise persons met everywhere—and that the recollection of these little episodes becomes, in their own minds, part of the ongoing story of the Santa Fe road.

What has occurred is that the present-day traveler has established a personal connection with the old trail and that connection is strengthened as familiarity grows. In time history to him may seem as real as his own experience. Although the age, the circumstances, and his perspective are far different, he is likely to develop a passion for trail life resembling that of the first generation of traders. In so doing, he yields to the alchemy of history and to the timeless urge lying buried deep in all of us to know where we have come from and how we became what we are.

To see that in its fullest dimension, we must turn now to the unvarnished details of life on the Santa Fe Trail in the wide lands beyond Council Grove.

FOUR

Into Peril and Hardship

I WAS DRIVING WEST ON US 56 as the sun's orange disc rose behind me flooding the prairieland ahead with radiant light. The night before in Council Grove the wind had blown gustily out of the southwest bringing with it a torrent of rain that pattered noisily against the window panes in my motel room. The sound had made me think of long-ago rains beating upon Osnaburg canvas that covered the Santa Fe wagons, and I was glad to be under a roof, not out on the open trail. But now, with the wide sky washed clean and clear, and with my spirits restored by the blazing sunrise, the road to New Mexico cheerfully beckoned anew.

Within a few miles past the Neosho, travelers had once upon a time spied their first herds of antelope, fleet and beautiful animals who provided fresh meat in abundance for the caravan hunters. But now all that I saw were occasional small herds of beef cattle, confined in tightly fenced pastures lining both sides of the highway. Since the disappearance of the antelope and the wagon trains, the land has shrunk. Barb wire and powerlines, farmhouses and fields have chopped up the space and confined the normal sweep of the eye. The transformation from a boundless plain to a rural landscape seems complete. The Santa Fe merchants would be hard pressed at present to find here anything they could recognize.

I am certain they would not be able to identify Diamond Spring, the first campsite out of Council Grove. To get there I turned south off the highway on a muddy country road and drove several miles to a two-story clapboard farmhouse framed by towering elms. No one was home except a pack of friendly hunting hounds. But I knew where to look for the spring, and I soon found it down behind the barn. My first view was an unsettling one. Gone was the "crystal fountain discharging itself into a small brook," as Gregg had described it. In its place was a little sinkhole containing a limpid puddle whose surface was coated with green scum. A large sheet of rusting corrugated iron covered part of the water. From the low, dark cavern it created, a bullfrog croaked a dismal welcome. I could see his tracks in the black ooze at the edge of the spring. My disappointment was tempered a bit by the thought that this had once been the most renowned watering spot on the entire Santa Fe Trail.

Commissioner George Sibley had given Diamond Spring its name during the government survey of 1825. Then, its still pure waters reminded him of a far-famed oasis in Arabia called Diamond of the Desert. Practically every keeper of a journal who passed by had some favorable comment to make about Diamond Spring. Around 1840 a thoughtful traveler implanted the root of mint in the moist bank. Thereafter, those who carried whiskey and sugar among their supplies were able to quench thirst with a cold mint julep.

But like every stop of note on the trail this one, too, had its moments of tragedy. Close by a caravan was caught in an early spring blizzard, and the men burned their wagons. For years afterward teamsters in need of chain, bolts, or other fittings picked through the rubble in search of something still serviceable. In fact, from this point forward, traveler Hezekiah Brake claimed to have seen tons of iron strewn along the Santa Fe road, "when for temporary relief from freezing men burned the woodwork of their wagons."

Since Diamond Spring was in hostile Indian country, campers here were occasionally assailed by war cries and arrows. In the autumn of 1852 a troop of soldiers stopped for the night on a little rise just east of the spring. Bands of Indians, thought to be Kaws, had been seen lurking on the column's flanks throughout the day.

The heavy grass, browned by frost, was powder dry, and the men took extra precautions in building their mess fires. Everyone with an ounce of experience knew what mighty disasters a careless spark could produce. Gregg tells of a novice cook with his caravan who "unwittingly kindled a fire amidst old grass" causing thereby a sudden prairie conflagration. The train narrowly escaped destruction and sight of the inferno racing toward the horizon, he says, was "sufficient to daunt the stoutest heart." Such fires, whether started by man or by lightning strikes, might consume enormous expanses of grassland before their progress was checked. Jim Beckwourth, carrying dispatches over the Santa Fe Trail in 1848, reported that the prairie was burned from Council Grove to Pawnee Fork, a distance of 150 miles.

Although the troopers at Diamond Spring that fall evening had exercised the proper care, they failed to reckon with the cunning Kaws. Supper was finished when suddenly fire broke out in a mile-wide circle around the camp. Flames, ignited by the Indians, leaped twenty feet high, entrapping the white men. Every hand grabbed a gunnysack or saddle blanket in a desperate struggle to beat back the blaze.

Sergeant Percival Lowe, recalling the incident, declared: "The utter destruction of our camp was imminent, and we faced the fire like men who had everything at stake. Success was ours, but the battle left its scars on nearly all. . . . My hands and face were blistered in several places; my mustache and whiskers, the first I had ever raised were utterly ruined. I dipped my face and head deep down into the lovely spring water to relieve the pain." Afterward, the suffering soldiers applied liberal portions of antelope tallow to their scorched flesh.

On another occasion driving the trail in eastern Kansas, I got a firsthand look at the awesome nature of a prairie fire. Topping the crest of a hill on the highway, I caught sight of a dense cloud of white smoke billowing along a three-mile front. As my car approached, the air grew hot and acrid. On the perimeter of the fire, men in line, working antlike, beat down the advancing tongues of flame with wet sacks. The scene brought to mind Sergeant Lowe and his companions at Diamond Spring who had been, in his words, "nearly blinded by smoke, heat, and ashes" before their efforts won deliverance.

One other potential source of trouble at the effulgent spring was rattlesnakes. Feeding on the tadpoles in the overflow pools, they proliferated. Seven-year-old Marian Russell, who strayed too far from her wagon in the 1850s, narrowly missed being struck by a granddaddy. "Superstitious folks in those days," she recollected, "believed that if you were bitten by a rattler and didn't die, every year at the same season you would break out in yellow and green spots like the splotches on the skin of a rattlesnake." Happily for her that bit of folklore remained untested.

Actually, rattlesnakes could be encountered almost anywhere along the way to Santa Fe. On the bald plains west of Diamond Spring, where rocks for chunking were not to be found, teamsters made sport of beheading rattlers with pistol, rifle, or the cracker on the tip of their monstrous bull whips. Before spreading blankets under a wagon at night, they made a wide circle to clear the area of any snake that might take a notion to share their bedding. Trail hikers and horsebackers at present find rattlesnakes just as disconcerting as did the original Santa Fe voyagers. Indeed, they pose one of the few dangers of prairie travel left over from the past century.

From Diamond Spring it was an easy day's march by wagon, slantwise in a southwestwardly direction, to the next campsite at Lost Spring. The water here came to life briefly beside the trail, flowed sluggishly for a short distance, then disappeared into the porous soil of the plain. Lost Spring was well named. To the traders its status was decidedly secondary; Gregg barely mentions it in his otherwise detailed itinerary.

The curious thing is that Lost Spring has retained much of its original isolation and charm, unlike Diamond Spring, so that now it is a superior spot, evoking the flavor of the trail era. A seldom-traveled county road provides easy access. Fifty feet or so north of that, the spring gushes into a pleasant pool tinged green in summer by lush grasses and sedges. A couple of historical markers are placed off to the side and do not intrude upon the picture-perfect scene. Today's visitor, unlike passersby of the last century, wants to linger for a while, knowing as he does, how rare are such unspoiled places.

The heat and humidity of an August afternoon had become decidedly uncomfortable when I turned my car into the gravel lane of Claude Unruh's farm, twelve miles beyond Lost Spring. Several people had told me, "Claude has the best watermelons in eastern Kansas. If you are going that way, don't fail to stop in." As it turned out, I was aimed in his direction anyway, because the Unruh fields lie upon the old caravan campground at the Cottonwood Crossing.

The Cottonwood, a tributary of the Neosho, was the first stream of consequence west of Council Grove. Its clean flow was not deep, but earthen banks on each side rose steeply from the water's edge making it difficult for the ungainly freight wagons to cross. Going down, wheels had to be locked and an extra ox team tied behind as a drag. Even so, spills were not uncommon. Moreover, the heavy work had to be accomplished in the evening when men and animals were bone tired from their day's travel. For the standard rule was that the fording should be made at once, not on the morrow. That way the train would not be held up in case a thunderstorm in the night made the banks slippery and swelled the stream to flood stage.

Claude Unruh was sitting under a tree in his front yard when I pulled up. A mound of cobalt green melons rested near his feet. Next to a For Sale sign was a small scale. "Take your pick" he said with a wave of his work-calloused hand, assuming that I was a customer. Quickly, I set him straight.

"Oh, so you are following the Santa Fe Trail," and he broke into a pleased grin. "Well, I know something about that. Look yonder across the road. You can see the wheel tracks coming down through that pasture. Then they disappear under my grain field on this side and show up again where the tilled land ends near the Cottonwood." And he added, "Come inside and I'll show you some relics I've plowed up over the years."

In his basement Claude Unruh had fixed up a small display. There were the usual arrowheads and other Indian artifacts, a buffalo skull, and a nice assortment of trail items—wagon parts, ox shoes, pieces of spurs, an 1835 half-dime, and a tarnished religious medal with raised letters reading *Mater Dolorosa* (Our Lady of Sorrows). The medal, I concluded, must have been lost by one of the many native New Mexicans who found employment on the trail.

Outside again, I walked down to the crossing now thickly clothed with timber and underbrush. With all the caravan traffic providing a constant demand for firewood, trees originally had been a good deal scarcer. Well after 1850, however, stands of cottonwood and willow could still be found. The stream got its name from the fact that this was the first place on the trail that the Plains cottonwood grew. Evidently tangles of fallen limbs and uprooted trunks tossed into jumbles along the shore inspired some early-day poet to contrive this bit of verse:

> The grand, majestic Cottonwood
>   Is neither slow nor swift;
> Its banks are lined with rotten wood
>   And other kinds of drift.

The flood debris, constantly replenished, furnished a ready source of fuel for camp cooks and probably explains why some of the living timber escaped the traveler's ax.

My prowlings about the ford inevitably brought to mind the names of some of those who had occasion to remember this location well. Among them was Manuel Alvarez, a native of Spain, long resident in the United States, who became prominent in the New Mexican trade and acted as American consul in Santa Fe from 1839 to 1846. In returning from New Mexico in November of 1841, one of his many crossings of the trail, Alvarez and his companions camped at the Cottonwood. His official report to the government tells the tale: "Same night had a severe snow storm, which continued for 48 hours with such violence we were unable to keep a fire. Snow 3 feet deep, we were all more or less frozen." In fact, two of the men perished as did most of the animals. That any survived at all was owing to Alvarez and another member of the train who braved the open plain to reach Independence and send back a rescue party.

A decade later Colonel Edwin V. Sumner with an army troop encountered an equally severe blizzard on the Cottonwood. He lost one man and nearly three hundred mules to the cold. If the crossing bore the reputation of an arctic hell in winter, it was well deserved.

Another traveler whose presence haunts the banks of this little stream is Susan Shelby Magoffin. When she arrived in late June 1846, the slope descending from Claude Unruh's present farmhouse down to the lip of the ford was a baize carpet of grass studded with tiny violet flowers, a far cry from the usual bleakness of mid-winter. Thickets of gooseberry, raspberry, and plum, their branches fruit-heavy and inviting, prompted the eighteen-year-old girl to ignore snakes and mosquitos and go gathering. The plums were still green, but, as Susan says, "I pulled some of them only to say I had picked three kinds of fruit in one spot on Cottonwood Creek."

The product of a sheltered life in a Kentucky manor, Susan had been a bride of but eight months when she set out from Independence with the caravan of her husband Samuel Magoffin, a veteran trader who was twenty-five years her senior. It was a journey destined to last more than a year, one that would carry her to Santa Fe, thence down the Chihuahua Trail to El Paso and across northern Mexico to the gulf coast and back, by sea, to the United States. The toll in hardship and disease would cause her death a short while later. But out of that raw experience came a daily journal rich in descriptions of trail life, of people met, and of the untamed countryside.

Susan's adoring spouse did his best to shield her from the rigors of the outdoors. She traveled in a Rockaway carriage accompanied by a servant girl. A variety of foods, including many delicacies, were hers. At night she retired to a capacious tent made comfortable with carpet, folding camp furniture, and a bed provided with a mattress and linen. Such luxury was unheard of on the Santa Fe Trail.

Yet, all of Samuel's well-meant efforts failed to keep harm and hardship from her pathway. An unkind fate dealt her plenty of both on the long miles of the trail. Although Susan was not free from complaining, here at the Cottonwood her forbearance and grit, extraordinary in one so young and untried, shine from the pages of her diary. In this instance it was the weather that challenged her good spirits, and she responded with girlish exuberance.

The trip from Lost Spring, punctuated by furious downpours, had been an ordeal. The road was a river of mud. Here and there wagons had dropped by the wayside as they became bogged to their axle hubs. One had its tongue twisted off as double teams, under the sting of the lash, tried to wrench the wheels free. Susan's light carriage and a companion supply-wagon managed to conquer the quagmires and reach a berth at the ford. But when her tent was raised, water covered the floor to a depth of several inches. Her bed she described as floating on a pond. And throughout the night gales and rain lashed the canvas above her head preventing sleep.

But when dawn brought a clearing of the skies, she informed her diary with renewed confidence, "It is truly fun for me." And on another page she wrote in neat script: "As bad as it all is, I enjoy it still. I look upon it as one of the varieties of life. If I live through this—and I think from all appearances I shall come off the winner—I shall be fit for one of the Oregon pioneers."

Evidently in the first couple of weeks on the trail, with her powers of tolerance stretched to new limits, she had grasped some of the possibilities that life in the open could offer. The road to Santa Fe might be a harsh taskmaster, but the compensations amply repaid the novice who showed resolve.

From the passage of the Cottonwood westward, a printed copy of Susan's diary rode beside me on the car seat. Driving over the plain I could sometimes, in my imaginings, glimpse her trail-worn Rockaway out front of the line of prairie schooners, the mules held in check so as not to outpace the slow grinding oxen. At those moments she was alive again, laughing brightly, calling to Samuel who trotted protectively nearby on horseback. Susan Magoffin herself, by some mysterious act of transplantation, had returned to the old trail, and part of the magic one senses traveling it now can be credited to her.

From the Cottonwood the wagonmasters followed a more or less direct line twenty-five miles down to Turkey Creek, so named for the immense flocks of wild turkeys roosting there. My own route, sticking to paved roads, proved a good deal longer. Along the way clusters of Kansas sunflowers filled the side ditches, imperceptibly moving their golden heads to face the course of the advancing sun. I've heard it said that the seeds became imbedded in mud caking the underbodies of the Santa Fe wagons and were carried all the way to New Mexico. There, where the sunflower had hitherto been unknown, they fell by the trail, took root, and blossomed. Today flowering ribbons of yellow that mark the wheel ruts leading toward the Pecos River seem to confirm the story.

After Turkey Creek comes the Little Arkansas, an inconsequential stream measured by the volume of its flow but looming large in the annals of the trail, owing to a tragic drama that began at its ford. I had been collecting details of the episode for a number of years, and they were in my thoughts as I hiked across a wheat field to the crossing. Swinging south of present McPherson, Kansas, the caravans were guided to this spot by a lone marker cottonwood tree visible far out on the plain. I found it easily, its forked trunk towering above neighboring timber that had grown up along the stream in the past half century.

On April 7, 1843, New Mexican merchant Antonio José Chávez arrived at this ford and cottonwood with the remnants of his bedraggled party. He had foolishly left Santa Fe for Independence in February, still well within the blizzard season. With him were twenty men, a female relation (Dolores Perea), two wagons, and about fifty-five mules. En route, stinging cold and fierce winds had pummeled the small cavalcade. Fifty mules perished and the majority of the group deserted, turning back toward New Mexico. At the Little Arkansas, Chávez was left with Perea and two or three servants. One of the wagons had to be abandoned and the other was piled with beaver pelts, gold bullion, and some silver coin to be used in making purchases in the Missouri markets.

Chávez was representative of the growing number of daring New Mexicans who had entered the international trade, purchasing goods at wholesale in Independence and Westport for resale both at home and in neighboring Chihuahua. Since the Mexican government levied lighter customs duties on its own citizens than it did on foreigners, they were able to undercut their American competitors and prosper. By 1843 several contemporary records affirm that the number of

New Mexico merchants traveling the Santa Fe Trail equaled or perhaps even exceeded the number of Yankees. They had become a major force in the overland commerce, and their business was much courted by wholesale houses in the United States.

For a number of years Antonio José Chávez had put in a regular appearance at Westport, and his arrival was always awaited with keen appreciation. In the spring of 1843, however, there appeared in that town one John McDaniel, an individual with a sinister air about him who claimed to carry a commission from the army of the Republic of Texas. For several days, McDaniel huddled over a table in Yoacham's Tavern on the Westport square, deep in conference with a dozen other dangerous-looking men. Eavesdroppers soon learned that the gang planned to invade the Santa Fe Trail and prey upon Mexican caravans. Pillars of the community at once sent word to nearby Fort Leavenworth, and a troop of dragoons was dispatched to intercept the raiders. But by then John McDaniel and crew were far out on the prairie and drawing near to the Little Arkansas.

Just west of the crossing, they came upon the hapless Chávez. He was instantly seized while the other members of the party were set afoot and told to go back to New Mexico. With their prisoner and his wagon, the bandits (for so they should be described) continued on the trail several miles to a small creek that meandered across the prairie. Here, after dividing up the booty, McDaniel announced that Chávez would have to be killed. About half his men objected, so they immediately departed for Texas. The remainder cast lots, and by that means it fell to McDaniel and Joseph Brown to carry out the murder. The poor trader was marched a short distance from camp and shot in the head. Then his body and the emptied wagon were dumped into a shallow ravine formed by the creek.

Merchant Ruben Gentry, returning from Santa Fe, arrived in Independence on April 19. He was the first to sound the alarm, reporting that the Chávez party, which had been traveling a few days ahead of him, had disappeared from the trail. At once the worst was feared, and the entire Missouri border was thrown into an uproar. Had harm befallen the New Mexicans, it might seriously disrupt the Santa Fe trade.

The Fort Leavenworth soldiers soon discovered Chávez's body, which they buried beside the creek. His wagon was brought into the settlements, and on the way his servants and Dolores Perea were found, wandering lost. The culprits had scattered through towns along the Missouri River, and within a matter of days about half of the gang was discovered and arrested. In a sensational trial the following year, McDaniel and Brown were convicted of the killing and were hanged in St. Louis before a huge crowd. Most of their accomplices received prison terms.

Later some of Chávez's relatives and friends set up a large stone as a monument at the site of his death. They also took back to New Mexico his wagon, retrieved for them by the military. Until recently, the remains of that wagon and a wooden strongbox that had carried the gold and silver were still in the possession of the Chávez descendants, who live on ancestral lands below Albuquerque. I saw the strongbox once, and it gave me a strange feeling to know that it had been present at one of the more somber events occurring along the Santa Fe Trail.

The little Kansas creek where the murder took place became known as Chávez Creek, but for unfathomable reasons the local folk had trouble saying that. Consequently, the name became corrupted to Jarvis Creek, and so it is shown on maps to this day. Sadly, the stone monument has long since disappeared, probably appropriated by an early farmer for a doorstep or foundation rock. Thus, no trace exists today along Jarvis Creek of the passing of Antonio José Chávez.

In spite of the Chávez incident, bandits were never a major threat to traffic on the trail. I can think of only a few other instances of outlawry—some attacks by border ruffians on the eastern end of the trail in the years just before the Civil War, and a couple of stagecoach holdups, one in Raton Pass and another in Glorieta Pass, during the 1870s. All of that was to the good, of course, because trekkers bound for New Mexico, or Missouri, had a multitude of other unpleasantries to deal with. Contending with bandits was something they willingly put out of mind.

The next major stream after the Little Arkansas was Cow Creek. Its deep and sluggish watercourse marked another boundary of sorts—the division between the tallgrass prairies, through which the caravans had been making their way since leaving the Missouri border, and the shortgrass plains lying beyond

The tallgrass, mainly bluestem, formerly covered some 400,000 square miles in the Corn Belt states of America's heartland. Horsemen on the Santa Fe Trail reported that the leaves came up above their stirrups and the seed stems reached six feet. Susan Magoffin, awed by the spectacle of boundless combers of tallgrass, likened the sight to "a waving sea of green." The plow and encroaching urbanism have reduced the tallgrass at present to no more than 4,000 square miles, a bare 1 percent of its original domain. Nice stands are still to be seen in the Flint Hills around Council Grove, and a few patches survive near the westernmost limit at Cow Creek.

But once over that creek, as the wagoners readily observed, the shortgrass took command, grama and buffalo grass principally. Here the thick herbage was measured in inches, not feet, which meant the caravans' draft animals had to range farther at feeding time. That presented a serious safety problem since the haughty Plains Indians at about this point became a menace to travelers. If the stock was not carefully guarded, a swooping raid could carry off the lot in a matter of moments. Beginning in the 1850s, U.S. troopers guarded the Cow Creek ford, and plentiful are the tales of lightning attacks and bloody repulses.

The vast expanses of shortgrass stretching toward the horizon meant one thing to meat-hungry travelers—buffalo! They roamed in herds by the thousands, grazing on blades and seedheads that cured naturally on the stem. On all sides the turf was cut by a myriad of narrow trails threading their way to watering places, and dried buffalo chips, the universal fuel of open country, dotted the plain. Some of the innocent young soldiers on Kearny's march of 1846 avowed they would not eat meat roasted over a dung fire, but since nothing but chips was to be had for cooking, the pangs of hunger quickly forced them to capitulate.

When the first buffalo herds were sighted, hunters from the trains went out on their fleetest hunting horses. Others, who could find a mount, joined in for pure sport. Once among the animals, the novices often became infected with "buffalo fever." They lost their heads and killed out of simple bloodlust. As a result, according to one Santa Fe traveler, the whole country approaching Cow Creek resembled "a slaughter pen, covered with bones, skulls and carcasses of animals in every state of decay." It was a case of abundance engendering wastefulness, a condition that frequently reared its ugly head on the American frontier. In any event, the supply of fresh buffalo hump and tongue was a welcome addition to the commissary, supplementing the usual trail fare of baked corn meal, bacon, rice, and beans.

Into the shortgrass country I drove past three low sandhills, known to the pilots as Plum Buttes, and continued due west to the Great Bend of the Arkansas. First sight of this river was apt to rouse the spirits of the men who came in rolling wagons, for as a popular refrain proclaimed:

> The Arkansaw, just half way
> From the States to Santa Fe.

Gathering its headwaters from the southern Rockies, the Arkansas slices across the southeastern quarter of Colorado and pushes languidly through western Kansas until, in about the center of the state, it curves northward in a wide, looping bulge to form its Great Bend. At the very top of that arc, the Santa Fe Trail made first contact with the river. Here, and for many miles above, the flow was shallow and turbid, wandering between banks a quarter mile wide and forming shifting islands of sand. For days ahead, extending beyond present Dodge City, the route stuck close to the valley and was guided by it.

Not far past the Great Bend, as the trail starts to slope toward the southwest again, the straining bull trains pulled up at Pawnee Rock, under whose shadow sprawled a favored camping ground. Although the highest point on the Santa Fe Trail east of New Mexico, Pawnee Rock, I suppose, would pass unnoticed anywhere except on the pancake plains of Kansas. A thumb of chocolate-colored Dakota sandstone, it juts from a low ridge forming the edge of the Arkansas's floodplain. A century back its flat summit rose above fifty feet, but later homesteaders quarried the rock unmercifully, so that now the feature is much reduced in both height and girth.

Nor was that the only loss. The sheer rock walls, stained black by iron oxide, presented a natural tablet upon which merchants, teamsters, and soldiers scrawled their names and the date of passing. Pawnee Rock thus became the unofficial register of the trail, where the famous and the obscure placed their autographs. Susan Magoffin did so on the Fourth of July, carving in haste while husband Samuel stood by fully armed, on guard against Indians. She mentions seeing hundreds of names, many of whom were known to her. But almost all have disappeared, including hers, victims of the rock cutters.

Samuel's vigilance was not unwarranted. The stretch of trail beginning at Cow Creek, reaching around the Great Bend to Pawnee Rock, and extending down to Fort Dodge has been dubbed the bloodiest ground in Kansas. Colonel Henry Inman, who traveled this road in its latter days, may have been indulging in a flight of poetic fancy when he said that every square yard of sod immediately below the rock contained the bones of a traveler massacred by Pawnee, Cheyenne, Kiowa, or Comanche. But the general meaning of his words—that the danger was acute and of long standing—cannot be disputed.

From the crest of Pawnee Rock, I gazed out upon wheat fields, past a grain elevator, to the now tree-lined margin of the Arkansas twisting lazily a mile or so to the south. Westward my eye followed a widening plain where earlier viewers had been able to pick out scattered herds of buffalo and antelope. Gone was the game, and gone, along this section anyway, were the deep wheel tracks of the schooners. I could still find, nevertheless, a gentle ridge running for several miles from Pawnee Rock down to little Ash Creek, one of the Arkansas's minor tributaries.

On that ridge one summer day in 1859 a host of befeathered warriors had lined up in attack formation, Hollywood style, as a wagon train of emigrants, heading for the Pike's Peak goldfields, moved along the trail a quarter mile below. Luckily, a cavalry patrol had just joined the caravan. It had been searching for these same miscreants who two days before had assaulted the Santa Fe mail coach, killing and scalping both driver and conductor.

The soldiers and emigrant men moved out from the wagons to form a defensive shield while the women and children, rifles at their sides, drove the oxen. The Indians clambered down the slope and rode back and forth in a fancy display of horsemanship, trying to draw the white men away from the train. The officer in charge, however, held his people in check. Against that resolute line of firearms, the warriors dared not charge. So they withdrew. "The women were brave and even the children were plucky," commented a young private with the patrol. But such successful confrontations with Indians in sight of Pawnee Rock were the exception and not the rule.

Travel at present seems so tame, in contrast to back then, that I sometimes wonder if we can ever fully appreciate what it meant to scan each crest of the plain in fear that just beyond, a scalping party was on the move. Those may have indeed been the "good old days," and an overland journey might well have provided a tempting way for persons of audacious spirit to escape from the humdrum. But the workings of fate were always ready to exact stern payment from the careless or from those whose courage faltered. If the days were truly good, it was because some men and women rose to the extraordinary challenge and faced the threats of the trail with a fearlessness that imparted its own sort of exhilaration. Recapturing even imperfectly a small part of that experience can tell us a great deal about the human condition.

There are two episodes involving Kit Carson that are supposed to have taken place in the vicinity of Pawnee Rock. Both, widely reported in trail literature, are said to have occurred on his first trip over the trail following his escape from the hated apprenticeship in Franklin. In one, the young, untested Kit was assigned to guard duty during the hours just after midnight. Hearing a noise beyond the perimeter of the wagons, he discerned what he thought was the shadow of an Indian and hastily fired into the darkness. Men leaped from their blankets and came running with a lantern. Investigation showed that Kit had shot his own saddle mule.

The trouble is that same story in later years was told of Jim Bridger and other mountain men—that each, on occasion, had killed his mount in the dark, mistaking it for an Indian. It was a stock yarn, utterly fictitious, and related in fun. Unfortunately, when it was told about Kit, the tale passed into the history books as straight fact. It is even mentioned on the historical marker to be seen along the highway just south of Pawnee Rock.

The second episode has some basis in fact. The principal version comes from Colonel Inman who knew Kit briefly and was, therefore, in a position to have gotten his information firsthand. According to his statement, while Kit's wagon train was camped between the Great Bend and Pawnee Rock, one of the teamsters suffered a severe wound in the arm when his musket accidentally discharged. It was clear that the mangled limb would have to be amputated. But no one was willing to attempt the disagreeable task until the boy Kit stepped forward and volunteered. Using a razor, a homemade saw, and a king-bolt heated white hot to cauterize the wound, the youth performed the operation with dispatch and the victim soon made a complete recovery.

Actually, the little drama unfolded just as Inman describes it, except in one important particular. Richard Gentry, a prominent Missouri trader, was the surgeon and not Kit Carson. Writing in his declining years, the colonel took unlicensed liberty in altering his story, no doubt to heighten reader interest by bringing in Kit's celebrated name. This incident, as well as the mule tale, demonstrate the rigorous winnowing necessary to get at the truth about the trail and those who followed it.

Kit Carson was at Pawnee Rock, all right, on his initial trip west, and on at least a half dozen subsequent occasions when he crossed the Santa Fe Trail. And sometime he must have carved his name on the stone register. If so, that invaluable inscription has been lost, along with Susan's and all the others. Yet, knowing he was here, one can still feel his presence. And that, too, contributes to the sphinxlike charm which persists in clinging to the historic rock.

Ten miles beyond in the town of Larned, I picked up my friend Earl Monger, a retired archeologist who has plotted every inch of the Santa Fe Trail between Pawnee Rock and Fort Larned. He guided me back to the unmarked site of the crossing at Ash Creek, a location that his own careful research had revealed.* The inconspicuous ford would not be worth searching out but for one small happening in the travels of Susan Magoffin. For it was here that her carriage, descending the dangerous, rutted bank, "whirled completely over with a perfect crash . . . [and was] entirely broken to pieces." Horrified, Samuel carried the stunned girl to the shade of a tree and revived her by rubbing whiskey on her hands and face. The accident undermined Susan's health and later led to a miscarriage at Bent's Fort. Earl and I agreed that even today the Ash Creek Crossing is a sad place.

The Santa Fe Trail as it exists today would be much diminished were it not for people like Earl Monger who, each in his own way, keep its historical memory alive. Hereabouts, community interest has been channeled into support of the Santa Fe Trail Center, a museum and archive quartered in a handsome building within sight of the Pawnee Fork, a major affluent of the Arkansas. I can usually find Earl there, working on exhibits or explaining the trail to visitors. He would agree with me, I believe, that the center, located close to the mid-point between Independence and Santa Fe, is now the heart and spiritual focus of the modern trail. It achieves that status in part because of the dedicated work of a host of volunteers, but also because it is the only facility along the route devoted exclusively to interpreting the chronicle of the Santa Fe Trail.

Driving up to the edge of the parade ground at the Fort Larned National Historic Site, three miles west of the center, my first impression was that a slice of the past had been frozen in time. That perception was owing to the authentic restoration of the nine stone and timber buildings in a quadrangle recently completed by the National Park Service. One can easily picture uniformed men swinging into regulation McClellan saddles and hear the clank of arms as they set forth on patrol. Founded in 1859, the fort was intended to protect caravans, stagecoaches, and mail riders on the eastern leg of the Santa Fe Trail. It also

---

*Recently Monger has installed a small historical sign to mark the crossing.

became a base for offensive operations against the southern Plains Indians and later guarded construction crews on the advancing Atchison, Topeka & Santa Fe Railroad.

In the ever-lengthening miles beyond Fort Larned, the contemporary traveler first begins to sense that he is entering the Far West. The land seems to stretch wider, with fewer man-made obstructions, and the sky arches higher with a greater clarity and deeper color. Official recognition of the transition can be found in Dodge City, the once glamorous cow town long exploited by Hollywood westerns and TV series. Next to the railroad station, a giant sundial marks the 100° meridian, an invisible north-south line that geographers acknowledge as the boundary of semiarid America. East of the line, rainfall is sufficient to sustain agriculture; to the west, it is deficient and irrigation is needed to bring in a crop. In trail days, overlanders referred to the country ahead as the Great American Desert, and they braced themselves for the sun-blistered hours and dry marches that awaited.

The old route, like the present highway, continues up the Arkansas Valley in the direction of Colorado. The barren expanses on either hand were vast, lonely, and overwhelming to easterners not yet grown accustomed to unfettered space. "Plain, plain, plain all the way. I am *so* tired of the plains," lamented George Willing in 1859. His mournful refrain finds an echo in the journals of many another wagon traveler. Josiah Gregg spoke of the melancholy that assailed him, while journalist Matt Field referred to the loneliness that afflicted every member of the caravan.

The mental stress was compounded by physical exhaustion that seemed to catch up with travelers in the outer reaches of Kansas. The hard daily drives beginning before the first blush of dawn and often extending past sundown left the teamsters fatigued. The night's rest, interrupted by guard duty, was never long enough to allow recuperation. Observed youthful Charles Raber on his first trip in the 1860s: "The most trouble we had was to keep the men from riding on the wagon tongues; they would go to sleep and fall off, thus getting run over." A New Mexican train heading east in 1867 had the same problem. Keeping eighteen-hour days, the drovers soon reached their limits of endurance. José Gurulé described the situation: "Too much awake. Too little water to drink. Too little frijoles. Men go to sleep anywhere." One of those who tried to catch a nap on his wagon tongue tumbled to the ground and was trampled to death by the frightened oxen. An exceedingly brief halt was called to attend to his funeral.

So, on and on the wagons went, their weary drivers maintaining a germ of optimism that, like a sinner's hope of heaven, they would somehow survive the multitude of threats to life and health, arriving at last unscathed in Santa Fe. And always in those interminable leagues west of Dodge City there was the dust—the inevitable dust. Hoof falls and churning wheels sent it skyward in powdery clouds, and in a thick blanket it settled again on everything—on face and hands, on black felt hats and hickory shirts, on canvas wagon tops, on the backs of mule and ox, on harness and yokes, and on the sun-bleached prairie grass. Dust salted the food and filled the lungs. It was the bane of all civilized men who treasured cleanliness. And it became thereby the most apt symbol and denominator of this stretch of the Santa Fe Trail that breached the sprawling plain and great desert—a metaphor for all that was unpleasant in the overland experience.

FIVE

The Forks of the Trail

A LITTLE MAXIM OF PYTHAGORAS, coined in antiquity, might easily have assisted the Santa Fe merchants, educated in the classics as many were, to make an important choice of routes on the far side of Kansas. For the old Greek had written: "Choose always the way that seems the best, however rough it may be." And, indeed, there was much to be weighed and pondered, regarding the best way, when a caravan came to the main forking of the Santa Fe Trail.

In the miles upriver from the future site of Dodge City existed several convenient crossings of the Arkansas, one of the favored lying just above the present town of Cimarron. The fording was made by those caravans electing to leave the river and strike out across open country on the shortest and most direct road to Santa Fe. This was the left-hand fork, if you will, the one called variously the Cimarron Cutoff, the Desert Route, or the Dry Route. The right fork, or longer leg that kept to the river well into Colorado, was known commonly as the Mountain Branch, or alternately after the mid-1830s as the Bent's Fort Cutoff. The parting of the two ways always presented something of a dilemma, because each road posed its own set of problems while at the same time offering travelers certain advantages.

During the first twenty-five years, the Cimarron Cutoff unquestionably enjoyed supremacy, carrying the bulk of the traffic. Not only was it one hundred miles shorter but the country traversed was wide and rolling with few natural obstructions for wagons. Even in that early day, time was money for the merchant capitalists so that the extra distance on the Mountain Branch, added to the herculean inconvenience of climbing Raton Pass, rendered the long Colorado route decidedly unattractive.

Yet, the Cimarron Cutoff had two clinkers, neither of which could be easily discounted. The first was a severe water shortage on the initial sixty-mile leg that reached from the Arkansas down to the Cimarron River. Experienced journeyers spoke of that drive as the most desolate stretch on the entire Santa Fe Trail, and in fact there was no other section to compare with it. The native New Mexicans called it the *Jornada*, a colloquialism in the Spanish of the Southwest meaning "a desert march." Americans, Gregg informs us, generally referred to it as the "Water Scrape." But from other sources we know that some of them attempted the Spanish name and pronunciation, mangling it in speech as "Hornally" and writing it with sharpened quills in their diaries as "Horn Alley." In either language, it was something to be dreaded.

Trail-wise captains were well acquainted with the Jornada's rigors facing their bull trains, and they took what limited measures were available to minimize the risks. Before leaving the Arkansas, five-gallon water casks, roped to the sideboards of the wagons, were filled to overflowing. Cooks prepared food for several days in advance. Men and animals drank all they could hold. Unless a chance thunderstorm formed a temporary pool in a buffalo wallow along the way, it would be the last water they would find for almost three days. The livestock bore the brunt of the hardship, and tales of mules and oxen dropping in their tracks from thirst were not unusual.

A prevalence of hostile Indians was the second strike against the Cimarron Cutoff. It led straight through the hunting range of the unpredicatable Comanche, Kiowa, and Apache. For brief intervals the tribes were at peace with trail travelers, but mostly their appetite for raiding was given free reign. Celebrated examples include thirty-three-year-old Jedediah Smith, foremost mountain man and western explorer, who was piloting a caravan across the Jornada in 1831 when he rode ahead alone in search of water on the Cimarron. Kneeling to drink from a pool, he was surprised by Comanches who ran him through with a lance. Farther up the cutoff, at the North Canadian Crossing just inside the modern New Mexico line, two young men named McNees and Monroe, out beyond their train, were set upon by unidentified Indians in 1828 and slain. To the west, at Point of Rocks in 1849, a small party was massacred by Apaches, and a woman and her infant daughter were carried into captivity. Beyond, near Wagon Mound the same year, Apaches and Utes waylaid the Santa Fe stage killing all eleven persons aboard.

Probably a five-pound book could be written recounting in gruesome detail the horrors of frontier conflict along the Cimarron Cutoff. But that hazard notwithstanding, men looked to their powder and their supply of lead ball and plunged headlong across the Arkansas and into the Jornada, because, as they kept reminding themselves, that was the quickest way to markets and profit, although it might just as well lead to an early grave.

By contrast, on the Mountain Branch, finding water and avoiding Indians were generally only minor concerns, although in the 1860s the once-friendly Cheyenne went on the rampage, menacing the commerce of the trail. Another draw, of course, was Bent's fur-trading fort on the north bank of the Arkansas, which long offered the only place to rest and resupply between the American settlements and New Mexico. That boon was denied those whose haste impelled them to opt for the Cimarron Cutoff.

But in 1846 two things occurred that prompted traffic to shift from the lower desert route to the upper mountain route. First, General Kearny and his Army of the West chose the longer way, mainly because Bent's Fort provided an excellent staging point from which to launch the invasion of New Mexico. His subsequent passage over Raton Pass with a large wagon supply train demonstrated to a merchant caravan in his rear the feasibility of surmounting that particular obstacle. And as noted, the army's march resulted in the removal of some boulders and a widening of the road in several especially difficult places.

Moreover, the summer of 1846 witnessed a withering drought across the Southwest. That made the Jornada even more painful and caused many of the scattered springs and waterholes beyond it to fail. Inevitably, wagoners exercised prudence and trailed on up the Arkansas Valley since some water could always be found there, even when the river sank beneath the sands, by scooping shallow wells in the bed.

For a spell in the 1850s, the Cimarron Cutoff regained a share of the traffic, but it was short-lived. The Pike's Peak gold rush of 1859 funneled a new tide of overlanders to Bent's Fort where they veered off the Santa Fe Trail and hastened on to central Colorado and the boom camps. Then, with the outbreak of the Civil War, Confederates from Texas were rumored to be prowling the Cimarron route and spoiling for a fight. That diverted still more caravans to the Mountain Branch, so that by the end of the war in 1865, it was being used almost exclusively.

On my own first trail excursion, when confronted with the forking of routes, I could pick the one that suited my whim of the moment for there was no need to dwell at length upon water availability, the Indian danger, or any burden an extra one hundred miles to Santa Fe might add. Since the Cimarron Cutoff, in the beginning, had been looked upon as the main trail, I elected to follow that, making a firm resolution in the same instant to return as soon as possible and do the Mountain Branch.

Once my car had cleared the Arkansas and the wide band of sandhills just beyond it, I emerged on the spacious plain and the start of the fabled Jornada. At once there came to mind Gregg's solemn remark that this featureless waste resembled "the grand prairie ocean," devoid of landmarks to help guide the way. Innumerable buffalo paths furrowed the land, alternately braiding together then unraveling, so that any novice who attempted to follow them in the hope that they pointed toward Santa Fe was soon utterly lost. This was no country for experimentation. The cardinal rule, formulated early on, accorded the best chance for safe passage: drive hard and fast in a direct line, southwest, until the Cimarron was struck.

I had a difficult time visualizing the Jornada in all its original, terrifying emptiness, so completely has the landscape been altered by progress in the twentieth century. Inside the neatly sectioned square-mile flats, man has drilled deep holes in the plains to tap the vast reservoir of the Ogallala Aquifer. The chug-chug of diesel pumps lifting irrigation water to tilled fields now assails the ears, dispelling the calm that trader Milton Bryan in 1828 likened to the noiselessness of the sleeping sea. And every so often, the blacktop highway passes through small farm towns with tree-vaulted streets and grain elevators topped by red beacons that wink in the night. One is scarcely aware, therefore, of passing through "a desert."

It was along the Jornada that men began to see mirages, a trick of nature that played havoc with the senses. "When your patience has been worn out by the long ride and when your lips are parched from thirst," relates Dr. Wislizenus in 1846, "there emerges in the plain before your astonished eyes a beautiful lake. Its surface looks like crystal. But the faster you hurry forward . . . the sooner you will be disenchanted. When you arrive at the very spot, you perceive nothing but the same hard, dry, parched soil over which you have traveled all day." The disenchantment of which he speaks was in itself part of the mystery and fascination freighters found in the trail.

Shimmering heat waves of summer probably played their part in the creation of mirages, or "false ponds" as Gregg called them. But the sheer immensity of the surrounding vistas also had a hand in distorting reality. Charles Raber said of the Jornada: "It is so level that in traveling over it one imagines himself in a basin, and looking in any direction the land seems to gradually rise until it meets the horizon." In this setting, travelers sometimes mistook a flock of ravens walking on the grass for a herd of buffalo, or a scattering of buffalo bones in the distance for an Indian war party. Young Raber, riding far ahead of his caravan, glanced back and was astonished to see the oxen walking on legs the length of telegraph poles and the wagons rolling high in the air. "It was a wonderful sight," relates he, "but soon faded away and left the train looking normal again." It was tales such as his that led those of romantic frame of mind to declare that the Santa Fe Trail was enchanted.

At the southern end of the Jornada, the thirsty caravans reached the lip of the plain, beyond which a sparsely grassed slope dropped gently to the naked banks of the Cimarron, an upside-down river, the wagon pilots called it. On this stretch, the bed was usually bone dry, but a few minutes digging in the alkali sand produced a natural well. Anywhere else, the chalky white substance that oozed into the hole would have been pronounced unfit to drink. Yet here, under the yoke of necessity, men and animals lapped it up eagerly.

Those who knew what they were about and possessed the services of an experienced pilot ordinarily managed to strike the Cimarron at the one point where fresh water was available. The Lower Spring (later renamed Wagon Bed Spring) gushed into a shallow pool a rifle shot above the river bank, then overflowed through a thatch of dark reeds and disappeared into the porous soil. From this place, the trail began to ascend the valley, keeping to the high ground as much as possible to avoid the buffalo gnats that swarmed in the bottoms. Thirty miles beyond was Middle Spring, another oasis, lying near a jutting bluff called Point of Rocks. It was the last major landmark before the Santa Fe Trail left the modern state of Kansas and entered the Oklahoma Panhandle, after just nicking the southeasternmost corner of Colorado.

At Willow Bar, named for a thick stand of willows, the trail left the river and for the next dozen miles bucked through the Cimarron Breaks, a scenic wilderness of hills, mesas, and canyons carved by small streams intersecting the route. Past Flag Spring and Cold Spring, the path emerged once more on the open plain. Not far beyond, the Santa Fe Trail skirted the site of Fort Nichols, a temporary post built and briefly occupied in the summer of 1865.

If I had to pick one landmark in Oklahoma that most vividly represented the spirit and drama of the trail in its latter days, it would be this one. Not much is left of the fort—a jumble of stones marking the outline of the 200-foot square walls and several rectangular depressions outside where the officers had their separate dug-out quarters. And the double-track, unimproved ranch road that brings you in is so punishing to motorized vehicles that all but the most determined visitor is turned away. Nevertheless, for those who know something of the history of this fort, it is a place not to be missed.

No other location on the entire trail, I believe, has kept its setting so unspoiled, unchanged. The 1860s here seem to reside in yesterday, not in the last century. On either side of the little promontory where the fort sits, two streams take their head, then enter wild canyons to the north draining toward the Cimarron. But on the south, the direction faced by the main gate, the pastureland rises in an unbroken sweep toward the sky's rim. A discerning eye can easily pick out, a mile away, the winding trace of the Santa Fe Trail, and sometimes even catch a glimpse of white-tailed antelope.

Colonel Kit Carson, then of the New Mexico Mounted Volunteers, is the chief name associated with Fort Nichols, for he was in command of the three hundred soldiers who marched eastward over the trail from Fort Union in May

1865 to build and man the walls. The remote outpost was intended to guard declining traffic on the Cimarron Cutoff at a time when all the southern plains were experiencing the ravages of a full-scale Indian war. Patrols from Fort Nichols escorted wagon trains and mail couriers east as far as Fort Larned and west to the security of the New Mexican settlements. That is, they rode escort until the end of summer when the fort was ordered abandoned. By the next spring, the main body of travelers had permanently deserted the Cimarron Cutoff in favor of the Mountain Branch, and the ruins of Fort Nichols were left in the backwash of history.

Although it is Carson's name that glitters, that of another shines from this bleak post with a glow that warms and illuminates the trail's story—Marian Sloan Russell. After marriage at age nineteen to Lieutenant Richard Russell, in the chapel at Fort Union, she came riding a dappled gray mare to spend her honeymoon and a summer's residence. She and her husband first lived in a tent a few feet west of the gate. Their bed was made of springy cedar boughs, the only real furniture an army camp table and a pair of folding stools.

Not far away was Colonel Carson's tent. On hot afternoons he rolled up the sides and lay on a cot scanning the horizon with field glasses. Once in the night a savage thunderstorm caught the fort in its path. Marian's description of the raging wind and the downpour are reminiscent of Susan Magoffin's experience while encamped at the Cottonwood crossing. Suddenly Kit Carson's howl of distress pierced the rain-swept darkness. His tent had collapsed, and he was trapped under the wet canvas. Lieutenant Russell jumped into his clothes and ran for the corporal of the guard. Together they rescued the commanding officer.

As construction of the fort progressed, Marian's tent was replaced by a dugout whose upper walls were masonry. It had a dirt floor and dirt roof with an army blanket for a door. Her diet was just as spartan: hard tack, beans, coffee, and venison or beef. One day when a freight wagon came from Fort Union, Richard bought his wife $42.00 worth of luxury eatables, including peaches at $2.00 a can. Within ten days everything had been consumed.

It was a sun-drenched day when I prowled through the ruins of the fort. I found the cavity in the ground edged by stones that had been Marian's dugout home and even picked up near the door a rusting and flattened tin can, its seams soldered with lead as was done in the 1860s, which could have held the peaches she ate. It was also possible to locate the spot where Kit's tent had stood . . . and fallen on that stormy night long ago. By the feel of the tin can in my hand, and the sight and smell of the place, I was making those direct connections with the past that I mentioned earlier, the ones that permit us to sense with vivid clarity the reality of the Santa Fe Trail experience.

For me, it is Marian Sloan Russell who provides the strongest tie and surest path to that world of wagon caravans now lost. Her little book of recollections

Land of Enchantment, dictated when she was in her nineties, captures and preserves for all time the very essence of life on the trail. For those modern critics and professional debunkers whose aim in writing is to proclaim that the western adventure was all woe, hardship, cruelty, and dirt, devoid of ennobling purpose and authentic romance, Marian provides a convincing antidote. She lived through the best and the worst of those times, survived them, and wrote about them with affection and sympathy. Since she was there and knew whereof she spoke, I choose to trust her judgment and pay heed to her observations.

As a lass of seven, in 1852, little Marian Sloan made her first journey over the Santa Fe Trail in the company of mother Eliza and brother Will. It was her introduction to the Great West and the rhythm of trailing, sometimes joyous and sometimes unnerving, as when she narrowly escaped a rattlesnake bite at Diamond Spring. On the Cimarron Cutoff, the girl gingerly gathered buffalo chips for the cooking fires, taking care to avoid the large spiders and centipedes that lurked underneath. But terrifying creatures notwithstanding, a love for the trail was born on that initial crossing, and it would stir in the blood for the rest of her life.

Widowed Eliza Sloan also succumbed to the plaintive call of the open road. Later, Marian would claim that her mother ripened into a true trail nomad who was never happier than when, on some pretext or another, she was traveling to and fro over the Santa Fe Trail. On that first journey west, the Sloans had set California as their final destination. But they got no farther than New Mexico. There, on an outside corner of the Santa Fe plaza, Eliza opened a boardinghouse in a dilapidated adobe building that had been part of the Spanish military presidio in colonial days. Archbishop Jean B. Lamy, long-distance trail rider François X. Aubry, and Kit Carson were often guests at her table. Sometimes Kit would take little Marian (he always called her "Maid Marian") by the hand and stroll with her about the dusty plaza. Years later he would attend her wedding at Fort Union and share the hardships at Fort Nichols.

After two years in the boardinghouse business, Eliza gathered up the children and joined a caravan returning to Missouri. That trip seems to have been the one that wedded her permanently to trail travel, for thereafter we find her constantly shuffling back and forth on the Santa Fe road. "It was the lure of the trail that drew her," Marian would claim. Happiness for Eliza Sloan had become reduced to a simple formula: endless rambling by a prairie schooner in the society of rough but courteous merchants, teamsters, and stock drovers. In reflecting back at the end of her life, Marian, who literally grew up under the billow and snap of wagon canvass, declared that she and brother Will, "came to love the feel of the grass under our feet and the sound of the wind and the waters. The trail [became] our point of outlook on the universe, the blue sky above us, bread and meat for our soul."

And she added with poignant eloquence, "If you have ever followed the old trail over mountains, through forests, felt the sting of the cold, the oppression of the heat, the drench of rains and the fury of the winds in an old covered wagon, you will know what I mean." There, in summation, is the inner meaning and the essential character of the trail experience. More than just a highway westward, the Santa Fe Trail offered a path to self-discovery and to a larger, fuller appreciation of nature's equation.

"It was strange about the prairies at dawn," recalled Marian. "They were all sepia and silver; at noon they were like molten metal, and in the evening they flared into unbelievable beauty—long streamers of red and gold were flung across them. The sky had an unearthly radiance. Sunset on the prairie! It was haunting and lovely." Others saw and responded to the trail's natural allurements, but few could describe them afterward with such sincerity and depth of feeling.

My visit to Fort Nichols put me in mind of the winsome Marian, and her words were much in my thoughts as I crossed from Oklahoma into New Mexico. Just past the state boundary, the old wagon tracks cut a wide swale through the crest of a rolling prairie ridge. Extra rainwater, collecting in the depression, had nourished a garden of bright green snakeweed that contrasted sharply with the short grasses on either side and plainly marked the course of the trail. I walked a short distance in the trench gouged by spoked wheels and wondered whether some of my footfalls were not landing on the same spot tread by the Sloans as they paced doggedly behind the moving tailgate of their wagon.

From this high ground I could look westward across scores of miles into the heartland of New Mexico. Conspicuous were several isolated mountains scattered on the horizon, the first to be encountered on this branch of the trail. All were known by name to the wagon pilots, and each served in turn as a guidepost by which the day's travel was directed and measured. Nearest at hand, to the lower left of my field of vision, were the twin peaks known as the Rabbit Ears. Beyond them about fifteen miles was the sloping hump of Mount Dora, and to its left the haystack-shaped Round Mound, now called Mount Clayton. And finally, indenting the skyline sixty miles or more to the northwest rose the lofty Sierra Grande. Trail chroniclers often spoke of these elevations as the beginning of the Rockies, whereas in fact they were separate volcanic intrusions into the plains, wholly unrelated geologically to the main chain of mountains beyond.

Later in the day, after skirting the Rabbit Ears, I turned off on a corrugated dirt road that took me close to the Round Mound. From the roadside a grass-carpeted plain stretched several miles to its base. I would have been tempted to make the hike but for the recollection of Josiah Gregg's experience. From approximately my same spot, several members of his caravan decided to walk what appeared to be the half mile or so to the Mound. To their astonishment, the distance proved many times greater, owing to what Gregg concluded was "an optical illusion occasioned by the rarified and transparent atmosphere of these elevated plains."

Finally gaining the top Gregg and his companions enjoyed an unsurpassed viewscape, more than a hundred miles in extent. Directly below them, the caravan could be seen widely dispersed, moving in four parallel columns and presenting "a very fine and imposing spectacle to those who were upon the summit." In open country, the wagon trains customarily traveled in that formation, not in the single line so often depicted by western films a century later. From this commanding vantage point, the men heard clearly "the unceasing 'crack, crack,' of the wagoners' whips, resembling the frequent reports of distant guns." And the lumbering white-topped vehicles suggested a picture of ocean-going ships under full sail. Years later, when he published *Commerce of the Prairies,* Josiah Gregg included an engraving, by way of illustration, of this very scene.

The next major landmark on the trail, New Mexico's Point of Rocks, lay twenty-seven miles ahead. The caravans steered toward it in an almost direct line from the Round Mound, but since today the country remains undeveloped ranchland without roads, I had to dip south to the highway, following a flat parabola that added many extra miles. When at last my route curved back to the foot of Point of Rocks, there again was my old friend, the trail, hooking in from the plain with a deep, bold track.

This rocky promontory, actually a warty digit jutting from the knuckled edge of a wide mesa, was a prime ambush site, popular with plunder-minded Apaches and Utes. Aware of that, the merchants as a rule circled their wagons a mile or so out on the flat and after camp was pitched drove the livestock under heavy guard to drink at the spring and pools lying beneath the overhanging cliffs. Sometimes the best precautions were not enough, and men died, struck down by arrows or bullets. The present owners of Point of Rocks, who have ranched there for years, drove me in their pickup to more than a dozen stone-mounded graves covering the bodies of travelers whose journey to Santa Fe ended here. The place still possesses a wild and desolate aspect, and one senses with palpable clarity the tragic side of the Santa Fe Trail saga.

In another twenty miles or so the trail reached the Canadian River at a place the New Mexicans called El Vado de Piedras, or the Stony Ford. A shelf of dull red sandstone spanning the shallow river bottom made an easy crossing for wagons, and driftwood carried down from the distant mountains by floodwaters provided an abundance of fuel for campfires. From the Canadian, a two-day march led to Santa Clara Spring in the shadow of the Wagon Mound, a towering bluff whose profile suggested a wagon top and the backs of oxen. Now the purple ramparts of the Sangre de Cristo Mountains, the southern extension of the Rockies, filled the horizon ahead and lifted the spirits of travelers who took the sight to mean that their weary trek would soon be at an end.

Not long afterward the wagon caravans arrived at La Junta, a campsite in an Elysian valley brimming with knee-high grass and furnished with groves of stately cottonwoods. The name La Junta had a double significance. Meaning "The Junction," it first referred to the union of the small, meandering Mora and Sapello rivers. But then with the opening of the Santa Fe Trail, the Cimarron Cutoff and the Mountain Branch, by coincidence, merged or rejoined at this same spot to become one road again for the final plunge to the New Mexican capital.

On the western arm of the trail, La Junta filled something of the same function that Council Grove did on the eastern. Located outside the line of settlement, it became a popular rendezvous site for overlanders preparing to return to the states. Lone travelers and small parties camped there until a large company could be made up or until a sizable train passed by, one strong enough to afford protection from roving Indians. Samuel Watrous came over the trail in 1849 and built a store and established a ranch at La Junta so as to profit from the constant flow of traffic. When the railroad built through in 1879, putting a finish to the trail, company officials changed the name of the place from La Junta to Watrous, the name it still bears.

After a brief tour of the historic La Junta, visiting a couple of markers and a nicely preserved stage station, I was obliged to do an about-face and head back to western Kansas and the start of the Mountain Branch. For no one can properly claim to have done the Santa Fe Trail until both its major divisions have been explored. Each has its own character and history which, united, round out the picture and complete the story.

I picked up the Mountain Branch near the site of an eminent landmark, Chouteau's Island. In its day it had been the largest island of timber anywhere on the upper Arkansas River. A heavy thicket of willows interspersed with cottonwoods had clothed its sandy surface. These woods had supplied shelter for fur trader Auguste Pierre Chouteau and several companions when they were attacked by Pawnees in 1816; hence, the name. A party of returning Santa Fe traders also took refuge here, in 1828, after losing their wagons to Indians down on the Cimarron Cutoff. Burying a heavy load of Mexican silver coin they had managed to save from the caravan, they slipped away on foot and finally reached Westport. The next year, a few of them returned to Chouteau's Island and recovered the treasure.

The island is gone now, long since swept piecemeal to the Mississippi by the Arkansas's spring freshets. But it was not hard to find the old location because a half mile due north rises a small oval mesa known as Indian Mound. Climbing to its brow, I could look over the valley and plainly see a long arc in the river, representing one side of the double bow that used to form the island. In a plowed field on my side of the Arkansas, a little hollow defined by a scatter of building stones was all that remained of the Bluff Stage Station, one of many isolated waystops for coaches that dotted the trail in its later years.

The Indian Mound is a good place to reflect upon the stagecoach and the part it played in the annals of the Santa Fe Trail. Under a canopy of dust, the ponderous Concord coaches and the lighter mud wagons, used in rainy weather, came careening and lurching up the Arkansas Valley filled with passengers, baggage, and the U.S. mail. Before 1861, they veered off opposite Chouteau's Island, if they had not already taken one of the other turnoffs downstream, and dived into the Jornada en route to the Cimarron. But early in that year, with the threat of Civil War looming, the Post Office Department moved the Santa Fe mail route from the Cimarron Cutoff to the Mountain Branch for safety's sake. It was never changed back, and as a result the longer road to New Mexico prospered from the service furnished during the main era of stagecoaching.

Initially, the trip from Independence to Santa Fe consumed about a month. For the $200 price of a ticket, passengers also received meals—mostly hardtack, bacon, and coffee, with an occasional addition of fresh game, if the messenger riding on top was a good shot. Everyone shared in the cooking and camp chores when the driver called a halt by the side of the trail to grab some sleep and rest the team of six mules. By the time the stages moved over to the Mountain Branch in the 1860s, regular stations began springing up every fifty miles or so, offering an improvement in meals and, at the ones designated home stations, a change of animals. Fresh mules also meant travel could be continued through the night, moon or starlight permitting. That nearly halved the time on the road.

From my perch on Indian Mound I studied the ruins of the Bluff Station where east- and west-bound coaches had rolled to a halt and discharged passengers for a brief stretch of the legs. A long, long ride in one of the jolting boxes was far from the romantic adventure that it has been pictured, and even a ten-minute breather at a small station like this one could feel like a gift from heaven. A full coach carried nine passengers inside, crammed three each in the front and back seats, and three more in the uncomfortable and backless middle seat, which was really a bench. Two additional persons could ride outside with the driver. Everyone went heavily armed in case of an Indian attack.

Besides the crowding, loss of sleep, monotony, and numbing cold (if the trip was made late in the season), the poor passenger had to contend with motion sickness. George Courtright was badly afflicted between the Bluff Station and Fort Lyon upriver. Lamented he: "I had never been sea sick, but was told the feeling is 'the victims wish to die.' However, nothing can be much worse than sitting both day and night in a stagecoach. What is known as 'coach fever' comes on accompanied with an excruciating headache, and every jolt of the coach is almost unbearable." A newspaper in one of the New Mexican settlements declared in 1875 that stage travelers on the trail were sometimes nearly "churned to death" before their ordeal was concluded.

As I continued up the Arkansas Valley in the cushioned comfort of my modern automobile, I almost felt guilty, knowing what misery the old Santa Fe Trail had put some of my predecessors through. I suspected that my view of the historic road might have lost some of its rosy tint had I been consigned to weeks in a stagecoach. Actually, stage passengers almost never praised the trail experience; that was left to caravan travelers who, like Marian Russell, found reward in the leisurely pace of the slow-moving oxen.

Not far across the present Colorado boundary, the Santa Fe road entered a precinct of the valley known to all plainsmen as the Big Timbers. A grove of mammoth cottonwoods, some of the trees seven to eight feet in diameter, extended thirty miles up the Arkansas. Cheyenne and Arapaho long used the area as a winter campground, and they, together with browsing game, kept the underbrush and smaller trees cleared so that the grove resembled an airy, well-shaded park. However, don't look for any of the original cottonwood monarchs now. The entire magnificent lot succumbed to the ax of goldseekers on their way to the Pike's Peak and Cripple Creek discoveries. The last tree is said to have come down in 1863.

The history of this section of the Arkansas, from the Big Timbers upriver to the point where the Santa Fe Trail finally left the valley for good, was long dominated by the activities of the traders William and Charles Bent. At the latter place, they built in 1833 their renowned adobe trading post, Bent's Fort. As headquarters for the largest mercantile firm in the Southwest, it had outlets at both Santa Fe and Taos. On the heels of the American conquest of New Mexico in the summer of 1846, Charles Bent was appointed governor, but the following January he died in a bloody revolt at Taos. Brother William, who had helped guide Kearny's invasion force from Bent's Fort to Santa Fe, tried to carry on the business activities of the firm, but with diminishing success. In 1849, he blew up the first fort, and moved thirty-eight miles down the Arkansas, to the lower end of the Big Timbers, where he built another post, called Bent's New Fort, on a bluff overlooking the gray green twisting of the river.

The morning was adazzle with Colorado sunlight when I found the New Fort, or what was left of it. Large heaps of stones outlined the perimeter of the walls, and a tall monument, as well as one of the small granite markers left by the DAR, confirmed that this was the handiwork of William Bent. He had struggled along here for a decade, trying to adjust to a faltering Indian trade and changing times. Then, he gave it up in 1860 when the army built Fort Wise (later renamed Fort Lyon) on the floodplain several hundred yards to the west. William leased his buildings to the government for use as a military storage facility, and twenty-seven years of commercial activity on the Santa Fe Trail by the Bents came to an end.

Looking down from the height near the monument to a tilled field and a cattle pasture abutting the river, I could see practically no trace of Fort Lyon. Flooding had caused its abandonment in 1867, and the military moved the garrison twenty miles upstream and built Fort Lyon II on higher ground. That afternoon I visited the second fort, which still exists, but as a veteran's hospital. Preserved on the grounds is a small rock building, almost a shrine, marking the spot where Kit Carson died in May of 1868. As I read a bronze plaque on the wall, it occurred to me how fitting it was that the winding trail, and indeed the entire western wilderness, had sustained him with "bread and meat for the soul."

On the road past the town of Las Animas, I came at last to the fairest and brightest jewel in the diadem of the Santa Fe Trail—Bent's Old Fort. It is not the fort the brothers built, for, as I mentioned, William destroyed that one. But rather it is a faithful reconstruction raised by the National Park Service in 1975–76 on the foundations of the original. Visitors must leave their cars out of sight and walk a quarter mile to the fort, a small concession that does much to preserve the proper historical atmosphere.

The massive earth walls; the round-bodied defensive towers; the rooms for trading, living, and storage—all properly supplied with period furnishings; corrals and stock barns; blacksmith shop; a large open courtyard adorned in the center with a cumbersome press for beaver pelts; and an outsized American flag floating above the sally port: it all rings so true that one can picture the Bents striding through the front gate and seeing nothing that is not as it should be.

Susan Magoffin at her first view declared that the complex "exactly fills my idea of an ancient castle." Adobe has that quality; a couple of years of weathering and it takes on the mellowed look of antiquity that stone needs several centuries to attain. An apartment in the upper tier of rooms was turned over to the Magoffins, and in the bed carried from her wagon Susan convalesced for more than a week. The accident back at Ash Creek had finally taken the life of her unborn child. Sadness and regret spilled over to her diary wherein she wrote, "I never should have consented to take the trip on the plains had it not been with the view and a hope that it would prove beneficial; but so far my hopes have been blasted." From Bent's Fort onward, her health remained delicate.

Within sight of the mighty fortress, the Santa Fe Trail forded the Arkansas River and pointed its course south and a little west toward the yawning gap of Raton Pass, nearly ninety miles away. The route led past Timpas Creek, Three Buttes, Hole-in-the-Rock, and Hole-in-the-Prairie. Throughout, wayfarers remained in sight of the distant Spanish Peaks. They formed the central feature in a panorama so breathtaking that no one traveling the road beyond Bent's ever forgot it. Seventeen-year-old Lewis Garrard, going this way early in 1847, was moved by the majesty of the twin peaks, "one beyond the other, rising until the furthest floated as clouds, their white crests apparently touching the sky." The unchanging Spanish Peaks represent one of those familiar landmarks that help preserve a continuity between yesterday and today for those retracing the trail. Their prominence in that regard was what led artist Thomas Hart Benton to give them a conspicuous place in his mural at the Truman Library in Independence.

Once arrived at the foot of Raton Pass, wagon trains camped outside the entrance alongside the noisy and diamond-clear Purgatory River, whose mountain waters delighted those who had wearied of the alkali drink forced on them in recent weeks. Lydia Spencer Lane, here with her husband's troop of soldiers on the way to Fort Union in 1866, called it "a pretty camp," a description which scarcely did it justice. The wooded river, luxuriant meadows, and pine-dressed walls of the Raton Mountains created a wilderness Eden unmatched by any other spot on the trail. The little city of Trinidad occupies the site at present. On a hill in one of its parks stands a heroic equestrian statue of Kit Carson. He is gazing intently toward the south and the dark cleft of the pass as if expecting to see one last caravan for Santa Fe enter and be swallowed up in the smoky haze.

Covered wagons and stagecoaches crawled over Raton Pass almost at the speed of cold molasses. Inside the narrow defile leading toward the top, the crack of bullwhips and the commands of teamsters had an eerie, muffled sound. At places, the path skirted dangerous precipices, and even seasoned hands momentarily held their breaths. "Worse and worse the road!" was how Susan Magoffin depicted her progress. And she tells of a dozen men laying hands on a wagon to steady it.

No real improvements showed in this troublesome piece of the trail until 1865 when trapper, freighter, and one-time hunter at Bent's Fort, "Uncle Dick" Wootton got a charter from the legislatures of Colorado and New Mexico to build a toll road. With a crew of workmen, he cut away hillsides, blasted rocks with gunpowder, and built bridges by the score. When all was competed, he installed himself in an adobe house next to his toll gate not far from the summit. Drivers on a new four-lane interstate can look down on portions of Wootton's road, a marvel of engineering in its day now shriveled to insignificance.

The far-reaching view of New Mexico from the crown of Raton Pass is among the choicest to be seen anywhere on the Santa Fe Trail. I paused at a turnout to take in nature's striking show and to gulp the sweet, thin air that makes respiration labored for flatlanders. To men and women who had been on the road for weeks, all the way from Independence or Westport or Fort Leavenworth, the overlook presented the prospect of an early end to their travels. Those who had made the trip before could point out to newcomers the distinctive line of the Wagon Mound etched against the sky seventy miles away. Near the foot of the Cimarron Cutoff, it stood as a sign that the convergence with the Mountain Branch was not far beyond.

Leaving the pass, the trail dropped swiftly to a plain, then ran in easy stages through the modern-day hamlets of Cimarron and Rayado. From the latter settlement, where Kit Carson farmed briefly in the 1850s, the route picked its way among a cluster of mesas and buttes to emerge finally at Fort Union, eight miles northeast of La Junta.

Gregg and many others of the trail's first generation never saw this huge military installation sprawling eventually over seventy acres of sandy grassland. Its founding did not come until 1851, six years after New Mexico passed into the hands of the United States. But later arrivals, like Marian Russell and her mother, grew to know it well, as did even a few of the aging veterans, Kit Carson and Dick Wootton, for example, who remained on the trail long after most of their early-day associates had departed. Fort Union fulfilled its double duty nobly, dispatching constant patrols as guardians along both branches of the Santa Fe road and also receiving army supplies from the East to be stored in its giant warehouses before dispersal to garrisons throughout the Southwest.

Although now a national monument, the stark ruins of old Fort Union have been left in as much a natural state as the canons of historic preservation will allow. And since swarms of visitors are practically unknown, it is possible for the modern overlander, just arrived off the Santa Fe Trail, to wander undisturbed over the spacious grounds. Like so many other out-of-the-way places tucked serenely into the folds of the trail, this one has preserved a timeless quality that reaches out and embraces all those who respond to the magic and excitement of the past.

I lingered several hours at the fort, walking far up the deep ruts of the Mountain Branch lying plain and open to the sky. But the end of the trail was calling, for Fort Union, now as then, is truly the gateway to Santa Fe. So with some eagerness, I headed out the paved access road on the last lap of my journey toward sundown.

SIX

"Santa Fe,
Oh, Santa Fe!"

WHEN ONE CONSIDERS THE MONUMENTAL CHANGES that have overtaken the world during the past century, it is remarkable to observe how few are the man-made additions to the landscape in the twenty miles between La Junta and Las Vegas. Beyond the barbed wire fences lining either side of Interstate 40, the outer fringe of the high plains remains empty and serene as it sweeps westward to touch the base of the Sangre de Cristo Mountains. Wagoners striding beside footsore oxen or stage drivers, high on their box, peered across this same distance looking for a far glimpse of Las Vegas, the first New Mexican town on the trail. But no early sighting was possible because the little settlement of adobe buildings, straggling around a large plaza, was hidden in a deep swale immediately in front of the mountain range.

I found the eroded scorings of wagon wheels on the downward side of the last ridge, so I left my car and followed them for a bit on foot. That allowed me to view Las Vegas, stretching below, from the same perspective as pioneer travelers. Since it now has population of more than ten thousand, perspective was about all I got in the way of an authentic look. People like Josiah Gregg or Susan Magoffin would have been hard pressed to envision a place, even of this modest size, in the future of the trail.

Las Vegas was founded in 1835 by twenty-nine Hispanic farmers and ranchers who obtained a land grant and brought their families eastward to this exposed frontier zone. The prime location, bestride the booming Santa Fe Trail, ought to have guaranteed that the new settlement prosper at once. But when General Kearny and his army passed by in 1846, it was still beggarly and uninviting.

Kearny and troops camped on a rise east of the plaza, a site now occupied by Highlands University campus. From there he rode to the open square, climbed to the flat roof of an adobe house, and read a proclamation claiming New Mexico for the United States. Listening below were the sullen men of Las Vegas. The women had been sent into hiding at El Crestón, a rocky ridge behind town. That was to prevent their being raped by the barbarian Americans and being branded on the cheek, as rumor had it, with the letters **US**, the same brand applied to army livestock.

Not until the 1850s did Las Vegas begin to emerge from its lethargy toward some kind of prominence. That was owing, quite likely, to the placement of Fort Union nearby, which put a check on Indian raiding in the surrounding countryside. Too, the new order brought a swelling of traffic on the Santa Fe Trail. In the post–Civil War period, more native New Mexicans entered the trade, forming huge trains at Las Vegas to transport wool to Kansas City and bring home manufactured wares much needed in the growing territory. Some of them employed experienced Anglos as mayordomos, or wagon bosses.

Two old Las Vegas families, the Bacas and the Romeros, emerged as leaders in this lucrative business. Few details are known of their methods of operation, but that they profitted handsomely was confirmed by their building of sumptuous mansions, replete with elegant furniture and glass window panes crated over the trail.

I spoke to an elderly lady of the Baca clan. Her grandfather, she told me, had died on the Cimarron Cutoff while returning from Missouri. In the vicinity of Cold Spring, he had come down with the dreaded cholera. A servant dosed him with the standard remedy—Penguin whiskey heavily laced with powdered red chile—but to no avail. The summer heat required a quick burial, but before that the body was soaked in a barrel of the whiskey. Primitive services concluded, the caravan resumed its progress.

Upon learning of the death of their patriarch, the Bacas were thrown into deepest mourning. That he had been left to lie in a lonely grave on the trail added to their distress. The following winter, when the temperature had dipped enough to permit the transport of a body, the Baca sons drove a wagon along the Cimarron Cutoff and, with the servant as a guide, located the grave site. Upon digging up the corpse, they discovered that the whiskey had perfectly preserved it. Back home, a proper funeral was held, and Señor Baca came to rest at last in ground consecrated by the church.

On Independence Day 1879, the first train of the Atchison, Topeka & Santa Fe (AT&SF) line came hissing and chugging into Las Vegas, all draped with patriotic bunting. Tracks had actually been laid a mile east of the plaza and a depot there became the anchor of New Town, or East Las Vegas, an Anglo suburb destined to grow and one day absorb Hispanic Old Town.

The coming of the railroad was the event that finally ended the trail story. But advance of the rails from eastern Kansas did not occur all at once. It was something that stretched over nearly a decade. And, in the process, the Santa Fe Trail went through one last phase of modification in both its character and route.

The impact of the railroad first made itself felt when the Kansas Pacific began building westward from Topeka in 1866, headed for Denver. By stages it reached Junction City, Ellsworth, Hays City, and, across the state line, Kit Carson, Colorado. Each place became briefly, in turn, the end of the line and the new supply point for New Mexico–bound caravans. The course of the Santa Fe road ran some miles south of the Kansas Pacific. But it was a simple matter to forge connecting links with the advancing railhead, thereby progressively shortening the number of miles freight had to be carried by wagon to Santa Fe. This meant that old, familiar places on the original route, like Independence, Westport, Council Grove, and Diamond Spring, had been left behind and were no longer part of the trail.

Another element entered the picture when in the early 1870s a new railroad, the Atchison, Topeka & Santa Fe, struck out from Topeka in a southwesterly direction, its sights firmly set on New Mexico. Following the wagon tracks of the Santa Fe Trail, it reached Dodge City in 1876 and, from there, elected to pursue the Mountain Branch on to Santa Fe. In weighing its choices, the company decided against the shorter Cimarron Cutoff, partly because the arid lands along that way could never be expected to attract a substantial farming population. And without people, there would be little demand for railroad services.

By contrast, the route up the Arkansas Valley to Colorado gave promise of one day becoming a prosperous agricultural kingdom. Added to that, the mountains surrounding Raton Pass were rich in coal and timber resources, coal being in demand to fire the steam engines and timber being needed for railroad ties. All those considerations outweighed the expected difficulties of construction over the pass.

The closer railheads of the AT&SF, of course, had taken the Santa Fe caravan traffic away from the Kansas Pacific. The Colorado towns of Granada, La Junta, and Trinidad each enjoyed a brief place in the sun as boisterous supply points where trail and rails met. All the while the old Santa Fe Trail was diminishing in length. When trains rumbled out of the south opening of Raton Pass in January 1879, what remained of the wagon road was entirely within New Mexico. Then, upon reaching Las Vegas on July 4 of that year, the railroad left the historic trail with only its last, paltry sixty-five miles.

By then most of the professional merchants and freighters had quit. What little wagon business remained was insufficient to keep them in the black. An exception was the firm of Otero, Seller & Company, headed by the redoubtable trader Miguel Otero. To the bitter end, he kept his caravans hauling goods from Las Vegas over Glorieta Pass to Santa Fe and down the Rio Grande to Albuquerque. Owing to his experience and resolve, Otero managed to squeeze a small profit out of the trail's last days. He may have gained a sense of personal pleasure as well, knowing that through him a long and respected tradition of freighting was coming to a close.

Miguel Otero and his hindmost wagon trains were much in my thoughts as I left Las Vegas heading toward Kearny Gap. Here, at the tail of my journey, I began to experience more strongly a nostalgic sense of loss for what once was, but is now gone forever. It was a somber emotion, but strangely one that also quickened the pulse and awakened me anew to pleasures available through immersion in history. By following the golden thread of the trail and reliving its past, I was led to feel, after the manner of Otero, that in some indefinable way I had identified myself with the tag end of a noble tradition. That perception caused me to remember the last lines of an old trail poem, and the words served to deepen the mood that had come upon me.

> So, when the night has drawn its veil
> The teams plod, span on span,
> And one sees o'er the long dead trail
> A ghostly caravan.

Leaving the interstate, I took what is locally called the Mineral Hill Road and shortly passed through the narrow defile of Kearny Gap, a natural cut in a one-hundred-foot-high volcanic ridge. The wagons had threaded their way single file, but once on the far side they moved out across a parklike valley in multiple ranks. From the exit of the gap, I observed the scarred ruts splaying onward like the ribs in a fan. Kearny had marched his battle-hungry men through this pass, expecting to be ambushed by Mexican soldiers that rumor said had been dispatched from Santa Fe to oppose his progress. But no enemy appeared.

In another eight miles or so, the trail wound past the native hamlet of Tecolote, whose founding dated from 1824. Sprawled on a red earth slope just north of Interstate 40, the rock and adobe houses spouting white smoke from their cooking fires still look much as they did a century ago. Only TV antennas and electric poles rising above the level of the rooftops mar the view and remind passersby that technology has intruded. Marian Russell and her husband had a trading post here in the year after his mustering out at Fort Union. As late as the 1960s, I was told, a portion of their ruined building could still be seen.

Beyond, the route climbs steadily, penetrating low forests of juniper and piñon pine and at certain high points presenting unobstructed panoramas of green-clad mesas and mountains. Leg-weary oxen and mules drew long breaths in the unaccustomed altitude and perhaps wondered, in their animal way, if this trip of nigh a thousand miles would ever end. Then some relief came at the summit of a divide, for the offside graded gently downhill several miles to the banks of the Pecos River and the town of San Miguel del Vado, St. Michael at the Ford.

Becknell landed here in 1821 and found a Frenchman in residence who could translate the words of Spanish officials giving permission to proceed on to Santa Fe, thereby opening the trail. Gregg, a few years later, thought San Miguel unimposing, saying that it consisted of irregular clusters of mud-wall huts. But as the Santa Fe trade expanded, the Mexican government installed a customs house in the town, along with a military garrison. That promoted both prosperity and population growth. Susan Magoffin in 1846 judged San Miguel to be larger and cleaner than communities previously seen, and she remarked favorably upon the church and plaza.

San Miguel appears three-fourths in ruins at present, and no one bothered me when I strolled the two blocks from the old church down a twisted lane to the river ford. Gregg described the Rio Pecos as "a silvery little stream which ripples from the snowy mountains of Santa Fe," and so it remains. I located a bevel in the bank that I was certain represented the site of the ford, even though the lower end of what must have been a dirt ramp had long since washed away in floodwaters. There is not much else to be seen, so only someone hooked on the trail and knowledgeable about what happened here would find anything to stir the imagination.

Soon after departing San Miguel, the Santa Fe Trail began another ascent, this one of about twenty-five miles to the top of Glorieta Pass. Except for an occasional shallow arroyo, the way was generally clear and the pull easy, at least when compared with the earlier haul over the Raton. Close by on the left, the solid wall of Glorieta Mesa rose abruptly to the sharp edge of its timbered rim, but to the right of the trail, toward the north, a wide bay pushed back the foothills, allowing splendid views of 12,000-foot peaks in the Sangre de Cristos. The caps of the far mountains glistened with snow as late as midsummer, gladdening the eye of travelers who had lately known the heat and thirst of the Jornada.

A few miles short of the Glorieta Pass, the trail made a swing that brought it past the thoroughly dilapidated walls of Pecos Pueblo and its ancient Spanish mission. Back in 1541, Coronado on his way to the Kansas plains had stopped by when the place, with a population of a couple of thousand Indians, looked a good deal more prosperous. But in the lapse of centuries between his visit and the advent of the Santa Fe Trail, Comanche raids and smallpox had taken a merciless toll. Seventeen years after William Becknell first saw Pecos, the few surviving inhabitants abandoned their homes and moved fifty miles across the Rio Grande to join their linguistic relatives at Jemez Pueblo.

Vacant Pecos Pueblo, forlorn and in ruins, became something of a tourist attraction for those journeying by wagon or stagecoach to Santa Fe. Since newcomers knew almost nothing of its history, they engaged in all sorts of fanciful speculations concerning the pueblo's origins and the customs of its former residents. Lieutenant W. H. Emory with the Army of the West recorded in his daily log one of the most popular yarns. "Here burned the eternal fires of Montezuma," said he, and when the last of the tribe left they took some of the live embers to Jemez, where "to this day they keep up their fire which has never yet been extinguished." How this chestnut about Montezuma's sacred fire got started is difficult to explain, but virtually every traveler who kept a diary made reference to it.

From Pecos, now tidily preserved and maintained as a national monument, I continued on a two-lane highway in the direction of the pass. Less than a mile from its summit, I stopped at Pigeon's Ranch immediately athwart the trail. Alexander Valle, alias "Pigeon," began farming at the site in the mid-1850s. He soon got a bigger idea and built a twenty-three-room adobe compound to serve as a hostelry accommodating traffic bound for the capital. It was here, in late March 1862, that Federal troops from Fort Union locked horns with Confederate invaders out of Texas. In what became known as the Battle of Glorieta Pass, or sometimes as the Battle of Pigeon's ranch, the Texans were turned back and New Mexico saved for the Union. Old Man Valle, of foreign origin, witnessed the fray and reputedly told an interviewer afterward: "Zey foight six hour by my vatch, and my vatch vas slow."

Three adobe rooms of the original complex still stand, but the rest is grassed-over mounds that give little hint of the true size and importance of Mr. Valle's establishment. Battle accounts say that the Confederate dead were stacked like cord wood to the ceiling in the ranch house, and I wondered if among the surviving rooms was the one that had doubled as a makeshift morgue. It was a grisly thought.

I recalled also that on the night of June 29, 1865, members of a touring congressional committee from Washington, gathering facts on Indian affairs, stopped to partake of Pigeon's hospitality. By chance, Kit Carson rode in an hour or so later. Having been relieved of his command at Fort Nichols a short time before, he was on his way home to Taos to see his family.

One of the members of the committee wrote of his pleasure in spending the evening with the renowned frontiersman. "Although about sixty years old, Carson does not look to be above forty-five," he noted. "We listened with great interest to his history of mountain life, his exploring and trapping expeditions, his Indian fights and bear hunts, told with a modesty and simplicity that carried conviction of the truth of all he said." Part of the charm of Pigeon's today, I had to conclude, lies in the fact that, "Kit Carson once slept here!"

Now it was less than twenty miles to the end of the trail and to the finish of a journey which for me had been a matter of days but for early travelers had consumed two and a half months or more. One final place of note was the site of the Rock Corral Stage Station situated ten miles out of Santa Fe. A. A. Hayes, a passenger on one of the last coaches to make the run from Las Vegas in advance of the railroad, remembered that "it was nearly dark when we changed horses at Rock Corral, and the stars where shining brightly as we looked down from the heights from which Mr. Gregg's wagoners [he had read *Commerce of the Prairies*] saw with delight the goal they were seeking."

In the years of Mexican rule, the caravans of merchants had been in the habit of pausing at an overlook above the capital to don clean shirts and slick down their hair. Past sufferings were about to be rewarded, and pride demanded that every man look his best upon the auspicious arrival. "It was truly a scene for the artist's pencil to revel in," intoned Josiah Gregg. "Even the animals seemed to participate in the humor of their riders, who grew more and more merry and obstreperous as they descended toward the city. I doubt, in short, whether the first sight of the walls of Jerusalem were beheld by the crusaders with much more tumultuous and soul-enrapturing joy."

The enormous freight wagons rolled down a dusty, narrow street (still today called Old Santa Fe Trail), lurched past the tower of the colonial San Miguel Chapel, and two blocks later emerged on the plaza, an arena presided over by the Spanish Governor's Palace that marked trail's end. Cheers burst forth spontaneouly, weather-stained hats sailed in the air, and one last cracking of whips resounded like a volley of rifle shots.

Before 1846 all goods had to be off-loaded at the Mexican customs house located on the northeast corner of the plaza opposite the palace. There they were examined and taxed before being released to their owners. At once the merchants went scrambling for shop space, the desired rentals being those facing the plaza. Manuel Armijo, the last governor under Mexico, even made available several rooms in one end of the palace as a way of lining his own pocket. Country merchants from outlying districts were on hand with the coming of each new caravan, so that trading got under way without delay.

The flock of teamsters, once they had seen to the delivery of their cargos, drove the emptied wagons several blocks south to the banks of the small Santa Fe River and a campground named, by local agreement, "The United States." Freed now from labor and schedules, they sought what delights this wild, unkempt town afforded. Fandangos, all-night dances where a stout drink known as Taos Lightning flowed freely, provided the first order of diversion. For those inclined to gamble, cockfights, horseraces, and tables dealing Mexican monte and three-card loo abounded. And of course there were ladies ready to greet the teamsters as if they were sailors in from the sea. Doña Tules, resplendent in silks and gold filigree, operated the best-appointed "house of pleasure" during the 1840s, and it was commonly accepted that she had briefly been the consort of Governor Armijo.

The opportunities for entertainment helped dispell the initial disappointment most new arrivals experienced upon observing the humble, even primitive face of the much-vaunted and legendary Santa Fe. Susan Magoffin expressed amazement at finding a cornfield growing close to the plaza and remarked disdainfully, "fine ornament to a *city,* that!" Rare was the American who failed to describe the buildings, constructed of unfired adobe blocks, as resembling brick kilns. And practically everyone took note that houses had floors of nothing more than packed dirt. Lieutenant Emory, however, admitted that though residences "are forbidding in appearance from the outside, nothing can exceed the comfort and convenience of the interior. The thick walls make them cool in the summer and warm in winter."

During the first quarter century of the trade, the town offered little in the way of civilized amenities to travelers. In the beginning, inns were nonexistent so that foreign merchants were obliged to sleep in their shops or spread blankets in the wagon camps by the river. Occasionally, the affluent ones rented a house for the season, like Samuel Magoffin, who found a plain, four-room adobe in which to accommodate the frail Susan.

Sometime after 1840 a most unpretentious hostelry opened for business on the outside corner of the plaza facing San Francisco Street. Known as La Fonda Americana, its few dingy rooms were quickly taken by traders with the year's first caravan. After the Kearny conquest, these lodgings passed into the hands of Americans who administered a facelift and changed the name to the United States Hotel. The man in the street, nevertheless, continued to call it La Fonda, even after another formal renaming made it the Exchange Hotel.

J. H. Beadle, a guest in the 1860s, found the Exchange to be "a one-story square" with a row of rooms containing the dining room and kitchen extending across the center courtyard, thus dividing the stable area at the rear from "the open court for human use" in front. "On the human side," he asserted, "men of quiet or literary tastes can sit and read; while the stable side is sacred to dog-fights, cock-fights, wrestling matches, pitching Mexican dollars, and other exclusively manly pursuits." Descending from his stagecoach in 1870, A. A. Hayes had nothing but praise for the hotel. "The air was balmy, the supper was good, and the residents sitting in and about this *fonda* seemed glad to see some new pilgrims arriving at the shrine of St. Francis," he wrote.

The gradual modernizing and Americanization of this hotel was a reflection of more sweeping changes that overtook Santa Fe in the decades after mid-century. While it cannot be said that Yankees entered in droves, once the town was theirs, those that did come were men of influence with their own ideas of progress. With the development of railroading, they perceived that bullwhacking on the Santa Fe Trail was fast becoming an anachronism, so they joined their voices with other leaders in the territory actively working toward introduction of the steam engine. One of them, William G. Ritch, warned tradition-minded citizens in 1879 that "they must adapt themselves to the situation by climbing out of the humble ruts of the old Santa Fe Trail to the higher duties resting upon and centering around the new and solid iron rail of the decade of the Eighties." His was the timeless call of men who seek to be in the forefront of change.

Heralding the new era by calling attention to the passing of the old, the capital's newspaper, the *New Mexican,* reported that on January 25, 1880, the firm of Barlow & Sanderson, which had long operated stagecoaches from the East, had suspended service, as of that date, on the last piece of trail between Las Vegas and Santa Fe. With rails nearly complete, its business was at an end.

The following February 9, the same paper announced "the coming of the Iron Steed and Santa Fe's triumph!" A great crowd of dignitaries and townsfolk assembled at the new depot several blocks south of the plaza to welcome the first train with flowery speeches and tumultuous cheers. And a large, black headline in the *New Mexican* announced with funereal finality: "The Old Santa Fe Trail Passes Into Oblivion."

So what had begun in 1821 with the quiet and unnoticed ride of William Becknell to Santa Fe, ended six decades later in glorious celebration and stirring rhetoric. Yet, as is often the case when one age closes and another opens, the shouts of approval can obscure the fact that with the gain, something is also lost. When the gate swung shut on the Santa Fe Trail, it sealed an unforgettable and incredibly picturesque chapter of our history. For those who lived through it and into the new day, the great adventure persisted as a treasured memory of an unrepeatable time. And they carried the imprint of that experience with them to their graves.

As exhilarating as had been my whole retracing of the trail from Franklin, nothing on the way quite matched the ultimate moment when, reaching the plaza, I placed my hand upon the polished face of the granite DAR marker that proclaimed the official end of the historic road to Santa Fe. I carried now the accumulated experience of my own prairie crossing, which had become intermingled at every stage with the warm recollection of numberless events, great and small, that composed the annals of the trail. The feeling which had first come upon me near Las Vegas returned: that by following in the wake of the prairie schooners and recreating in my mind's eye the pictures of the past, I had somehow managed to tether myself to a luminous history, one replete with deep and intimate meanings. If that sounds pretentious and unlikely, I can only suggest that finding the universal is oftentimes easier through attention to the particular and personal.

Sitting on an iron bench near the End-of-the-Trail marker, I basked in the pleasure of my own small accomplishment and in the suffused glow that derives from being elbow to elbow with history. The Santa Fe plaza, laid out by colonial Spaniards in 1610, has stood witness to practically the full range of human achievement, tragedy, and folly. Royal governors, the king's soldiers, Franciscan padres, aristocratic dons and their elegant ladies in silk mantillas, sheepherders, and beggars once walked this ground. The summer of 1680 saw the plaza besieged by Pueblo Indians in bloody revolt and the turquoise sky above obscured by the smoke of a burning town. Much later, in 1844, surly Utes from the Rockies were here to bargain for peace with the Mexican governor. When negotiations broke down, the melee that ensued left Indian bodies strewn in front of the palace. Memory of that unsavory fray was still fresh in residents' minds that August 18, 1846, when General Kearny, backed by troops bristling with weapons, raised the American flag to the roar of a thirteen-gun artillery salute.

Today, the environs of Santa Fe, in proper push-ahead Yankee fashion, are being paved, malled, and subdivided to death. But around the plaza, the municipal nerve center, a carefully tended facade of antiquity remains. We Americans love quaintness—as long as it can be made to pay and doesn't intrude upon our beloved creature comforts—and the Santa Fe plaza is above all quaint, with its monuments and tree-shaded open space, bracketed on every side by porticoed buildings in Spanish or territorial style. Yet, the bow to the demands of tourism aside, there are enough lingering traces of the past to make this a very special place for those wishing to drink from history's well. The bit of verse that follows was penned by a bard who listened on the plaza and caught the faint echoes of another time.

> Santa Fe! Oh, Santa Fe!
> Your call I ever hear;
> Santa Fe! Old Santa Fe!
> Your voice is always near.

On my bench, lost in reverie, distant voices seemed to amplify in volume, so that gradually it was not hard to imagine that I could eavesdrop on the likes of Becknell, Gregg, Carson, Kearny, and the Magoffins. Here, they, and all the rest, had walked and sat, talked and perhaps reflected how each in his own way, pursuing his own separate destiny, had helped swell the sail of history on the road to Santa Fe. Upon entering the limitless prairie west of Independence, Susan Magoffin had exclaimed in delight, "Oh, this life of mine I wouldn't exchange for a good deal." And, the very same sentiment, we know, animated many others who braved the overland journey that brought them at last to this sun-drenched plaza.

That we have so much in the way of elemental knowledge about their doings and motives is attributable to the large quantity of diaries, journals, and narrative accounts, published and unpublished, left to us. It is as if, in their enduring monuments of words, the writers of the wagon age were attempting to reach beyond their own brief moment in time and establish communion with a remote future, the shape of whose new orders they could scarcely conceive. It is the unspoken desire of all authors that when each dies and his familiar world disappears, his book continues to live. In following the Santa Fe trail with a dozen of those books in hand, I had vicariously entered the realm of caravans and stagecoaches, joining with the original participants in forging a bond between past and present. Therein, I had to conclude lay the incomparable lure of the trail, the source of the pull that placed one irredeemably under its magical spell.

"There have been many things in my life that I have striven to forget, but not those journeys over the old Santa Fe Trail," spoke Marian Russell in her own memoirs. "My life as I look back seems to have been lived best in those days on the trail." Some of her looking back had been done from an iron bench next to the DAR marker, for at ninety she had returned to Santa Fe to revisit the plaza where, as a small girl, she had ambled hand in hand with Kit Carson and, still later as a new bride, had linked arms with her Lieutenant Russell. It was June 1932, and Kit's little Maid Marian was the last living person who had traveled the trail in the 1850s and 1860s and who had known his touch and the sound of his voice.

In dreamily casting backward, she wrote with poignant intimacy: "The inner chamber of my heart is open wide, its pearls of memory just inside. My thoughts move slowly now like motes behind a faded window blind. I stand listening for the sound of wheels that never come. The voices I loved ring from afar. My heart has returned to the land the old trail ran through, so long ago."

So, Marian Russell too is gone. Now the Santa Fe Trail belongs to the keening wind. It belongs to summer rains and to the fearful snows of winter. It is owned by the prairie dog, the jackrabbit, the rattlesnake, and by an occasional antelope. It is the property of the roadrunner, the mockingbird, and the soaring nighthawk. And for a brief interval it is mine, by adoption, since I choose to stake my claim to a tiny fragment of its shining history. On the plaza, I strain, as Marian did, to hear the distant noise of spoked wheels clattering down the trail's last mile and the pop of the ox-drover's whip. But nothing like that is in the air. Those sounds, once real, are no more, and they will not come again.

Sources

CHAPTER ONE

FOR THE GENERAL HISTORY of Old Franklin, I have relied upon volume 3 of Louis Houck, *A History of Missouri* (Chicago: R. R. Donnelley & Sons, 1908); Anonymous, *History of Howard and Cooper Counties, Missouri* (St. Louis: National Historical Co., 1883), especially chapters 6 and 7; and, W. F. Johnson, *History of Cooper County, Missouri* (Topeka: Historical Publishing Co., 1919). From the last named source (p. 158) comes the quote, "It had sprung into opulence. . . ." The quote from the *Missouri Intelligencer* appears in Larry Beachum, *William Becknell, Father of the Santa Fe Trade* (El Paso: Texas Western Press, 1982), 12. On John and Bailey Hardeman, see Nicholas Perkins Hardeman, *Wilderness Calling* (Knoxville: University of Tennessee Press, 1977). The verse beginning "So hold your horses, Billy" is recorded by W. W. H. Davis, *El Gringo: or, New Mexico and Her People* (New York: Harper & Brothers, 1857). For Kit Carson's boyhood in Franklin, refer to M. Morgan Estergreen, *Kit Carson, A Portrait in Courage* (Norman: University of Oklahoma Press, 1962).

CHAPTER TWO

Indispensable for an understanding of both early Independence and Westport is Anonymous, *The History of Jackson County, Missouri* (Kansas City: Union

Historical Co., 1881). I also found useful W. L. Webb, *The Centennial History of Independence, Mo.* (Independence: privately printed, 1927); Pearl Wilcox, *Jackson County Pioneers* (Independence: privately printed, 1975); and Walker D. Wyman, "Kansas City, Mo. A Famous Freighter Capital," *Kansas Historical Quarterly,* 6 (Feb. 1937), 3–13. On the mural and the artist's background, see the pamphlet by Thomas Hart Benton, *Independence and the Opening of the West* (Independence: Harry S. Truman Library and Museum, 1974); and John A. Diffily, "Thomas Hart Benton, An American Regionalist," *Southwestern Art* 9 (May 1980), 106–13. Augustus Storrs's report from the Congressional Record has been reprinted several times, notably in Archer Butler Hulbert, ed., *Southwest on the Turquoise Trail* (Denver: Denver Public Library, 1933), 77–98. Records of the Sibley survey appear in Kate L. Gregg, ed., *The Road to Santa Fe* (Albuquerque: University of New Mexico Press, 1952). Senator Benton's advocacy on behalf of western trails is described in most general histories of the pioneer movement, and in William Nisbet Chambers, *Old Bullion Benton* (Boston: Little Brown and Co., 1956). For Missouri steamboating I relied heavily, although not exclusively, upon Erik F. Haites, James Mak, and Gary M. Walton, *Western River Transportation* (Baltimore:John Hopkins University Press, 1975); and W. L. Campbell, "Steamboating in the Santa Fe Trail Days," *Westport Historical Quarterly* 1 (Aug. 1965), 3–5. The quote, "Westport was full of Indians . . . ." is by Francis Parkman and appears in William R. Bernard, "Westport and the Santa Fe Trade," *Transactions of the Kansas State Historical Society* 9 (1906), 560.

CHAPTER THREE

Much of this chapter was inspired by Josiah Gregg's *Commerce of the Prairies* (Norman: University of Oklahoma Press, 1954), and all of my direct quotes by Gregg here and in later chapters are taken from it. The reference to Gregg by Paul Horgan appears in his book, *Josiah Gregg and His Vision of the Early West* (New York: Farrar Straus Giroux, 1979), 11.

For general background on Council Grove, I have used Lalla Maloy Brigham, *The Story of Council Grove on the Santa Fe Trail* (Council Grove: Morris County Historical Society, 1921); and Margaret Whittemore, *Historic Kansas* (Manhattan, Kansas: Flint Hills Book Company, 1974).

Quotes by the following authors will be found in the places cited: William R. Bernard, "Westport and the Santa Fe Trade," *Transactions of the Kansas State Historical Society* 9 (1906), 559; that by Matt Field in John E. Sunder, ed., *Matt Field on the Santa Fe Trail* (Norman: University of Oklahoma Press, 1960), 70; Adolphus Wislizenus, *Memoir of a Tour to Northern Mexico* (Washington: Tippin & Streeter, 1848), 6; and George D. Brewerton, *Overland with Kit Carson* (New

York: Coward-McCann, 1930), 283. The quote beginning "A dream of picturesque . . ." comes from Hezekiah Brake, *On Two Continents* (Topeka: Crane & Company, 1896), 176; and another, "The air . . . is many times clearer . . .," appears in Frank H. Trego, *Boulevarded Old Trails* (New York: Greenberg, 1929), 31. Franz Huning's views of the trail are contained in Chapter 2 of his grandson Harvey Fergusson's book, *Home in the West* (New York: Duell, Sloan and Pearce, 1944). The quote from the *American Review* is cited in Stanley I. Kutler and Stanley N. Katz, eds., *The Promise of American History* (Baltimore: John Hopkins University Press, 1982), 45.

CHAPTER FOUR

The several quotes relating to Diamond Spring, beyond those of Gregg from his *Commerce of the Prairies,* are cited as follows: Brake, *On Two Continents,* 130; Jim Beckwourth on the prairie fire, from Marc Simmons, "The Santa Fe Trail, Highway of Commerce," in *Trails West* (Washington: National Geographic Society, 1979), 28; reference to the Kaw attack and Percival G. Lowe's comment are found in his *Five Years a Dragoon* (Norman: University of Oklahoma Press, 1965), 110; and Marian Russell, *Land of Enchantment* (Albuquerque: University of New Mexico Press, 1981), 67.

Clyde Brion Davis records the quatrain about the Cottonwood in *The Arkansas* (New York: Farrar & Rinehart, 1940), 11. Manuel Alvarez's trip is described in Alvarez Claim, no. 66, Records of the Department of State, Claims Against Mexico, National Archives. The blizzard that struck Colonel Sumner and his men is mentioned by Hobart E. Stocking, *The Road to Santa Fe* (New York: Hastings House, 1971), 99. For Susan Magoffin's experience at the Cottonwood, see her diary edited by Stella M. Drumm, *Down the Santa Fe Trail and into Mexico* (New Haven: Yale University Press, 1926), 23–29.

The Chávez murder receives passing comment in a number of contemporary souces, including Gregg's book. But as yet, no monographic study of the complete episode has appeared. Basic details are available in *Niles National Register,* various dates for April and May 1843; and in Maurice Garland Fulton and Paul Horgan, eds., *New Mexico's Own Chronicle* (Dallas: Banks, Upshaw and Company, 1937), 130–35.

The quote describing the buffalo range as "a slaughter pen" is drawn from Robert Selph Henry, *The Story of the Mexican War* (Indianapolis: Bobbs-Merrill Company, 1950), 127. The Arkansas couplet appears in Kenneth L. Holmes, *Ewing Young, Master Trapper* (Portland, Oregon: Binfords & Mort, Publishers, 1967), 12. The comment about the bravery of the women and children was made by Private John S. Kirwan, "Patrolling the Santa Fe Trail," *Kansas Historical*

Quarterly, 21 (Winter 1955), 583. Colonel Henry Inman's accounts of Kit Carson's supposed adventures at Pawnee Rock are located in Chapters 16 and 20 of his standard work, *The Old Santa Fe Trail* (Topeka: Crane and Company, 1899).

George Willing's lament about the plains occurs in his "Diary of a Journey to the Pike's Peak Gold Mines in 1859," *Mississippi Valley Historical Review* 14 (December 1927), 363. For the remark by Charles Raber, see, "Westport, Missouri in the 1850s, "*Westport Historical Quarterly* 7 (March 1972), 11. José Gurulé's recollections of life on the trail are in Typescript No. 48, WPA Files, History Library, Palace of the Governors, Santa Fe.

CHAPTER FIVE

For general information on the Cimarron Cutoff and the Mountain Branch I have used R. L. Duffus's standard work, *The Santa Fe Trail* (New York: Longmans, Green and Co., 1931). The Wislizenus quote is from his *Memoir of a Tour to Northern Mexico,* 11–12. Raber's remarks about the Jornada come from his article, "Westport, Missouri in the 1850s," 10–11. The history of Fort Nichols is summarized in Albert W. Thompson, "Kit Carson's Camp Nichols in No Man's Land," *Colorado Magazine* 11 (July 1934), 179–86. All quotes by Marian Sloan Russell in this chapter, and the one that follows, are drawn from her book *Land of Enchantment,* edited and recorded by Mrs. Hal Russell (Albuquerque: University of New Mexico Press, 1981).

For the mechanical details of the history of stagecoaching, I have relied upon Morris E. Taylor, *First Mail West, Stagecoach Lines on the Santa Fe Trail* (Albuquerque: University of New Mexico Press, 1971). George Courtright's description of his stage sickness appears in his small booklet, *An Expedition Against the Indians, 1864* (Lithopolis, Ohio: privately printed, n.d.), 2. The news account telling of stage passengers being "churned to death" is cited by William A. Keleher, *The Fabulous Frontier* (rev. ed.; Albuquerque: University of New Mexico Press, 1962), 21. Susan Magoffin's statements are taken from her *Down the Santa Fe Trail and Into Mexico,* 60, 64, 80. Lewis Garrard's description of the Spanish Peaks is in his *Wah-to-yah and the Taos Trail* (Norman: University of Oklahoma Press, 1955), 129. Lydia Spencer Lane's quote is cited by James W. Arrott, *Brief History of Fort Union* (Las Vegas: privately printed, 1962), 10–11.

CHAPTER SIX

For the early years of Las Vegas and surrounding country, I leaned on two local histories: Milton W. Callon, *Las Vegas, New Mexico* (Las Vegas: Las Vegas Publishing Co., 1962); and Lynn Perrigo, *Gateway to Glorieta* (Boulder, Colo.: Pruett Publishing Co., 1982). The story of Señor Baca's death on the Cimarron Cutoff was related to me in 1979 by Fabiola Cabeza de Baca. The coming of the railroad is described in most general histories of the trail, including Dufus, *The Santa Fe Trail*, 257–67; and Seymour V. Connor and Jimmy M. Skaggs, *Broadcloth and Britches: The Santa Fe Trail* (College Station: Texas A & M University Press, 1977), 180–95. Useful also on this subject is Glenn Danford Bradley, *The Story of the Santa Fe* (Boston: Gorham Press, 1920).

The verse beginning "When the night has drawn its veil" is quoted by Margaret Long, *The Santa Fe Trail* (Denver: W. H. Kistler Stationery Company, 1954), 3. Material on Otero, Seller & Co. appears in Miguel Antonio Otero, *My Life on the Frontier, 1864–1882* (New York: Press of the Pioneers, 1935). Susan Magoffin's remarks about San Miguel and Santa Fe are noted in her *Down the Santa Fe Trail and Into Mexico*, 98, 103. Lieutenant Emory's comments about the Pecos fires and his description of Santa Fe are recorded in Ross Calvin, ed., *Lieutenant Emory Reports* (Albuquerque: University of New Mexico Press, 1951), 53–54, 60. Ralph Emerson Twitchell in his *The Leading Facts of New Mexican History* (reprint ed., 2 vols.; Albuquerque: Horn and Wallace, 1963), II, 384n, quotes Alexander Valle on the Battle of Glorieta.

Reference to Kit Carson at Pigeon's Ranch is found in Lonnie J. White, ed., *Chronicle of a Congressional Journey* (Boulder, Colo.: Pruett Publishing Co., 1975), 44. Remarks by A. A. Hayes on the Rock Corral and La Fonda come from *New Colorado and the Santa Fe Trail* (New York: Harper & Brothers, 1880), 159. J. H. Beadle tells of the plaza and La Fonda in *The Undeveloped West* (Philadelphia: National Publishing Co., 1873), 449. The quote by William G. Ritch is given by Terry Lehman, "Santa Fe and Albuquerque, 1870–1900," (Ph.D. diss., Indiana University, 1974), 133.

For details of the arrival of the first train in Santa Fe, see, Paul A. F. Walter, "The Coming of the Railroad," *El Palacio* 39 (July 1935), 2–4. All quotes by Marian Russell in this chapter, as noted, are drawn from her *Land of Enchantment*, while an account of her last visit to Santa Fe was printed in the *New Mexican*, June 8, 1932.

Along the Santa Fe Trail

Old Franklin, Missouri, 1983

The town of Old Franklin, the original starting point for the Santa Fe Trail, was washed away by the flooding of the Missouri River in 1828. On the spring day when this photograph was taken, the site was again under water.

Boone's Lick, Missouri, 1983

Daniel Boone's sons boiled water from a salt spring in kettles to obtain salt in the early nineteenth century. William Becknell worked on a salt-making crew and departed from the vicinity of Boone's Lick on his first trip over the trail in 1821.

Arrow Rock, Missouri, 1983

When William Becknell returned here after his first trip across the trail, he split open
his saddle bags and let the Mexican silver coins tumble into these stone gutters.

Sappington Cemetery, Missouri, 1983

In these impressive iron-bound tombs lie Dr. John Sappington and his wife Jane. Dr. Sappington developed a pill containing quinine to prevent malaria. His "anti-fever pills" were carried by many travelers departing for Santa Fe.

Fort Osage, Missouri, 1983

Fort Osage was established by William Clark in 1808 as a military garrison and Indian trading post. It was from here that the Sibley Survey left in 1825 to mark the Santa Fe Trail.

Polly Fowler, Independence Landing, Missouri, 1984 (*opposite*)

Independence was the primary outfitting point for the Santa Fe Trail from its founding in 1827 until the 1850s. Behind Polly Fowler, who is the local expert on the history of Independence, is the bluff that new arrivals by steamboat climbed on their way from the landing to Independence Square.

Westport Landing, Missouri, 1983 (*above*)

By 1850 the trail head had moved westward to Westport. The industrial bustle of Kansas City has obliterated all traces of the old steamboat landing and warehouse area.

Rice Plantation, Missouri, 1983

Archibald Rice's farmhouse was an early stopping place along the trail. The log house belonged to Aunt Sophie and is one of many such slave cabins that once ringed the plantation.

110-Mile Creek, Kansas, 1983

This surviving stage station building with three sides of stone and one of wood was built by Fry McGee about 1854. Today, it lies abandoned in the middle of a plowed field.

Havanna Stage Station, Kansas, 1983 (*opposite*)

Dragoon's Grave, Kansas, 1983 (*above*)

A few miles west of Burlingame, Kansas, are the beautifully cut limestone walls of a stage station, the only remains of a small town of German and French immigrants founded in 1858. Across the modern highway is the grave of dragoon Samuel Hunt who died along the trail in 1835.

Kaw Commissary, Council Grove, Kansas, 1982

The Kaw Indians signed a treaty in 1825 guaranteeing safe passage of the Santa Fe caravans through their country. They received their annuities in this stone building which now lies forgotten southeast of town.

Roe Groom, Kansas, 1984 (*above*)

Council Grove, Kansas, 1982 (*opposite*)

The town of Council Grove was the last source of hardwood for the repair of wagons heading west. The trail crossed the Neosho River on the site of the present-day bridge and followed Main Street through town. Roe Groom walks sections of the trail every year to raise money for the Arthritis Foundation and knows exactly where the trail passed through the Council Grove area.

Last Chance Store Window, Council Grove, Kansas, 1982

This small stone building built in 1857 was the last place to buy supplies for westward-bound caravans. It has been preserved and now stands silently alongside the trail in a residential neighborhood.

Lost Spring, Kansas, 1982

Lost Spring is a heavily wooded, undisturbed trail site. A New Mexico cowboy won this spring, along with a store and a saloon, in a poker game in 1866 and stayed two years.

Sarah at Durham, Kansas (near Cottonwood Crossing), 1982

"The camp ground is on a slight rise, and some three or four hundred yards down is a steep bank covered with cottonwood trees. . . . Just at the water's edge are quantities of gooseberry and raspberry bushes. . . . Above these on the side rather of the cliff, is a thick plum grove . . . I pulled some of them only to say I had picked three kinds of fruits in one spot on Cottonwood creek" (Susan Magoffin, 1846).

Cow Creek, Kansas, 1983

This photograph was made in a light drizzle very early on a spring morning. Cultivated fields and oil and gas wells obliterate most of the early trail ruts in Kansas, but it is still possible to locate springs and creek crossings.

Pawnee Rock, Kansas, 1982

Pawnee Rock was a prominent landmark and favorite Indian ambush site. Unfortunately, the top of the hill which had been covered with extensive early trail inscriptions was quarried for the building of a railroad and homes.

Larned, Kansas, 1983

Fort Larned was established by the army in 1859 to protect trail travelers. Buffeted by fierce blizzards of the plains, sun-roasted in summer, and often threatened by hostile Indians, the post offered no easy life for troopers. Today it is operated by the National Park Service.

Ash Creek Crossing, Kansas, 1983 (*above*)

Earl Monger near Kinsley, Kansas, 1983 (*opposite*)

An archaeologist with the Santa Fe Trail Center in Larned, Earl Monger is an expert on the several branches of the trail in Pawnee County. He stands in the ruts of the trail near the Kinsley crossing of Coon Creek.

Lower Spring, Kansas, 1982 (*opposite*)

Lower Spring Marker, Kansas, 1982 (*above*)

This site on the Cimarron River was a lifesaver for traders who had traveled the dry
forty miles from the Arkansas River. In 1831, famed Indian scout Jedediah Smith was
killed by Comanches while searching desperately for this spring. The trough (left) running
vertically up through the grasses is the Santa Fe Trail. The red granite stone (right) was
one of many markers erected by the Daughters of the American Revolution to mark the
trail at the beginning of this century.

Middle Spring, Kansas, 1982 (*opposite*)

Upper Spring, Oklahoma, 1982 (*above*)

The few springs along the normally dry Cimarron River were oases to travelers after long days on the dusty plains. "It was on the last day of June that we arrived at the 'Upper Spring.' . . . The wildness of this place, with its towering cliffs, craggy spurs, and deep-cut crevices, became doubly impressive to us, as we reflected that we were in the very midst of the most savage haunts" (Josiah Gregg, 1831).

Fort Nichols, Oklahoma, 1982

Kit Carson commanded this small stone fort in the Oklahoma Panhandle for three months in 1865. Today it is an undisturbed and isolated trail site with an exhilarating, unobstructed view of deep ruts from the old road.

Inscription Rock, Oklahoma, 1982

What a different sense of time in the nineteenth century—travelers made the effort to carve beautiful graffiti! This sandstone bluff contains many early inscriptions and is so isolated that it has not been defaced in modern times.

McNees Crossing, New Mexico, 1982

The wagons crossed dry, sandy Corrumpa Creek on a shelf of sandstone and cut this deep trench in the banks where they ascended. The crossing was named after a young trader who was shot and killed by Indians as he napped after lunch.

Turkey Creek, New Mexico, 1984

"The approach to this Creek, particularly with the Waggons, was a little troublesome on account of the numerous ridges & hollows that interpose. We got down very well however, and halted at a small grove of Cotton Trees opposite a high Cliff of Rocks, where we found very excellent Water, Grass and Wood. The Water is in Pools" (George Sibley, 1825).

Rabbit Ears Creek, New Mexico, 1982

Because the Rabbit Ears Creek campground provided abundant wood, grass, and game, caravans often lay over here for several days. Ruts of the trail can be seen entering and departing from the lovely open meadow above the spring.

Round Mound, New Mexico, 1982

Round Mound was a major landmark for wagon trains. Often trail travelers scaled the summit and described the sight and sounds of the caravan passing below: "The wagons marched slowly in four parallel columns, but in broken lines, often at intervals of many rods between. The unceasing 'crack, crack,' of the wagoners' whips, resembling the frequent reports of distant guns . . ." (Josiah Gregg, 1831).

Krystal at Point of Rocks, New Mexico, 1982

A fine spring in a deep canyon made Point of Rocks a favorite campground despite frequent Indian attacks. Teepee rings from Indian encampments and rock-covered graves of massacre victims can still be seen.

Dorsey Mansion, New Mexico, 1983

This salamander fountain is part of the landscaping for the lavish mansion built by New Mexican politician and swindler Stephen Dorsey in late trail days. Today the blowing wind and passing thunderstorms are the only guests at this abandoned site of yesteryear parties.

Bent's Old Fort, Colorado, 1983

In early trail days this adobe trading post, built in 1834, was the only structure between Missouri and the little Spanish towns near Santa Fe. The fort sits like a castle with its rounded turrets on a bluff overlooking the Arkansas River; one can easily imagine Indian encampments spread over the plains beyond it. When travelers crossed the Arkansas River just southwest of the fort, they headed into what was then territory of the Mexican Republic.

Bent's New Fort, Colorado, 1983

William Bent abandoned his original trading post in 1849 and built a new fort about thirty miles down the Arkansas. This second fort was built of stone and has not been restored like the earlier adobe trading post, Bent's Old Fort.

William Bent's Grave, near Boggsville, Colorado, 1983

Freighter, trader, and friend of the Indian, William Bent was closely identified with the Mountain Branch of the trail during the last half of his life. The monument over his grave is seldom visited today.

Boggsville, Colorado, 1983

This home belonged to J. W. Prowers, an early Colorado pioneer, and was a stage stop. Unfortunately, the photograph cannot convey the raucous conversation of hundreds of blackbirds that often roost in the trees.

Iron Springs Stage Station, Colorado, 1983

The stretch of trail between Bent's Fort and Trinidad was long and barren in the ninteenth century and remains so today. These post stubs are all that remain in the rectangular corral that enclosed the station's livestock.

Raton, New Mexico, 1982

Until a toll road was built in 1866, the Raton Pass on the New Mexico border was a formidable barrier to wagon travel. Travelers descending the mountains had this view of the volcanic landscape of northeastern New Mexico.

Ocaté, New Mexico, 1983

From the top of Apache Mesa one has a grand view of the eroded ruts of the trail as they swing down from Rayado between two mesas, circle around the tip of Apache Mesa, and then head toward Fort Union.

Wagon Mound, New Mexico, 1982 (*above*)

"The road passes at the foot of the so-called Wagon Mound, which I ascended as far as the rocks would allow . . ." (F. A. Wislizenus, 1846).

Les Vilda, New Mexico, 1984 (*opposite*)

With his burro, Joker, Les Vilda and three friends walked the entire Santa Fe Trail from Fort Osage to Santa Fe in the summer of 1984.

Fort Union, New Mexico, 1982

Fort Union was the major army garrison serving the western section of the Santa Fe Trail. What remains today on an empty prairie are the ruins of brick fireplaces, adobe walls, and cut stone walkways. Only the stone jail has survived structurally intact. Radiating from this old fort are clearly visible ruts, silent evidence of the heavy traffic once seen on the Santa Fe Trail.

Masonic Temple, Watrous, New Mexico, 1982

Watrous, or La Junta as it was originally called, was first settled by Samuel Watrous in 1849 and was the junction of the two branches of the trail, the Cimarron Cutoff and the Mountain Branch. This abandoned lodge was one of the earliest Masonic structures in New Mexico and served some of the soldiers from Fort Union.

Livery Stable, Watrous, New Mexico, 1982

According to some reports, this building also once housed a saloon. Today it is empty and rapidly deteriorating; several of the adobe sides have floor-to-ceiling cracks, and the roof is beginning to collapse.

Tecolote, New Mexico, 1982

". . . The day warm and pleasant, and we had nothing of interest, passing through the miserable Town of Tuckelota" (G. R. Gibson, 1848).

San Miguel, New Mexico, 1983 (*above*)

San Miguel, New Mexico, 1981 (*opposite*)

This town with its lovely church was the site of customs collections for caravans entering Mexican territory. The trail crossed the Pecos River and entered the plaza opposite the church. Today, when the bell in the church courtyard is rung, its sound reverberates among the buildings of a nearly deserted town.

San José, New Mexico, 1982

San José has a beautifully preserved Spanish plaza with adobe houses encircling the square and the church in the center. This photograph was taken through the ruins of a mercantile building; a single plume of smoke was the only indication of present human activity.

Pecos, New Mexico, 1981

Pecos contains the ruins of a Spanish mission church and an Indian pueblo. It was a romantic last-night camping spot for travelers on their way to Santa Fe.

Pigeon's Ranch, New Mexico, 1983

Only three rooms remain of what was once an extensive hostelry built by Alexander Valle in the 1850s to cater to Santa Fe Trail travelers; indeed, Kit Carson spent a night here in 1864. Recent restoration work has momentarily saved the small building from collapse.

Cañoncito, New Mexico, 1981

Cañoncito figured conspicuously in the Civil War Battle of Glorieta Pass. The Union forces slipped behind the Confederate front line and burned the enemy's supply wagons here. The battle proved the turning point of the war in the West.

San Miguel Church, Santa Fe, New Mexico, 1984

"My expectations of seeing a fine city had already been cooled down by previous accounts of travellers, and by the sight of the Mexican country towns through which we had passed. However, when I perceived before me that irregular cluster of low, flat roofed, mud built, dirty houses, called Santa Fe, and resembling in the distance more a prairie-dog village than a capital, I had to lower them yet for some degrees" (Frederick A. Wislizenus, 1846).

Santa Fe Trail Entering Santa Fe, New Mexico, 1984

Modern Santa Fe retains the adobe architecture that surprised and dismayed early trail travelers. The Yankee merchants with their teamsters, oxen, and wagons are gone. Yet the historic streets and old plaza still bustle, as artists mingle with descendants of Spanish colonial settlers, and Pueblo Indians hawk their wares in the open air to throngs of tourists.

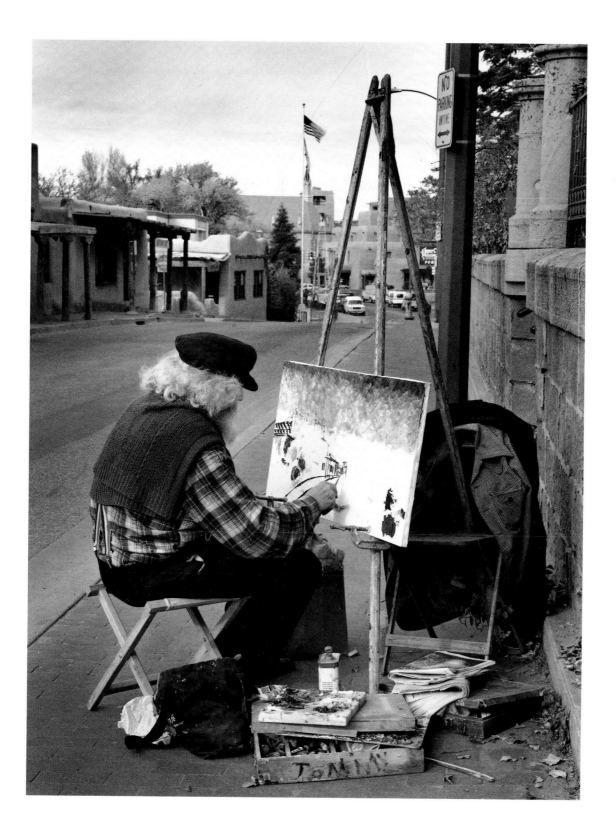

ALONG THE SANTA FE TRAIL
was designed by Emmy Ezzell,
and typeset by the University of New Mexico
Printing Plant in Goudy Old Style.
The duotone plates were printed by offset lithography
in Japan by Dai Nippon Printing Co., Ltd.
The text was printed at Thomson-Shore, Inc.,
and the books were bound
by John H. Dekker & Sons.